THE ART OF MAKE-UP
FOR STAGE, TELEVISION AND FILM

THE ART OF
MAKE-UP

FOR STAGE, TELEVISION AND FILM

VLASTIMIL BOUBLÍK

TRANSLATED FROM CZECH BY
BOHUŠE ČERNOHORSKÁ-VOLFOVÁ

LINE DRAWINGS BY
A. MICHALČÍK

THE QUEEN'S AWARD
TO INDUSTRY 1966

PERGAMON PRESS

OXFORD · LONDON · EDINBURGH · NEW YORK

TORONTO · SYDNEY · PARIS · BRAUNSCHWEIG

Pergamon Press Ltd., Headington Hill Hall, Oxford
4 & 5 Fitzroy Square, London W.1

Pergamon Press (Scotland) Ltd., 2 & 3 Teviot Place, Edinburgh 1

Pergamon Press Inc., 44–01 21st Street, Long Island City, New York 11101

Pergamon of Canada Ltd., 207 Queen's Quay West, Toronto 1

Pergamon Press (Aust.) Pty. Ltd., 19a Boundary Street, Rushcutters Bay, N.S.W. 2011, Australia

Pergamon Press S.A.R.L., 24 rue des Écoles, Paris 5ᵉ

Vieweg & Sohn GmbH, Burgplatz 1, Braunschweig

First edition 1968

Library of Congress Catalog Card No. 68–18519

FILMSET BY THE EUROPEAN PRINTING CORPORATION LIMITED DUBLIN IRELAND
PRINTED IN GREAT BRITAIN BY D. R. HILLMAN & SONS LTD., FROME

08 012651 0

CONTENTS

CONTENTS

INTRODUCTION

PERFECT make-up is a very important and indispensable part of the actor's performance in the theatre, in film and in television. I have been working on this book for a number of years in an attempt to make a survey of today's knowledge and experience and present a complete picture of the situation of contemporary artistic make-up. I have been influenced most in my work by the atmosphere and environment of the film studios. In justification for devoting most of this book to film, I should like to mention that film makes the greatest demands upon the skill and artistic imagination of the make-up artist and upon the make-up itself.

V. BOUBLÍK

Prague, 1966

1. MAKE-UP THROUGH THE AGES

IT IS very difficult to say when people started to use make-up. It is quite certain, however, that it must have been a very long time ago and it was probably due to an urge or longing on the part of human beings to change the world around them.

Ever since ancient times people have been preoccupied with their appearance and have always tried to improve their looks and enhance their physical charms; it is here that make-up has always been a vital factor, guided and influenced from the very outset by fashion, and dependent on it.

Fashion has changed countless times through the ages, making inevitable changes in the methods of make-up. The purpose of make-up today is no different from what it has always been, namely a desire among humans to improve their beauty. Apart from this, however, present day make-up has another aim—to counteract the harmful effects of rough weather, working conditions and irritating air-pollutants.

Modern cosmetics, containing biologically active components, have gradually replaced the former aids, i.e. charcoal, pigments, animal and vegetable juices and extracts, etc.

Methods of make-up at first in the theatre, later in the film industry and now in television are also changing according to fashion. However, the most decisive influence upon make-up is due to artistic and technical development in this art. Stage and screen make-up has always been an important factor in the artistic performance of the actor.

The development of theatre make-up has a very long and interesting history.

In ancient Greek dramas there was only one actor—apart from the chorus—and he played several parts. Later on there were two actors and in the second half of the fifth century B.C. there were three actors who played the various roles in turn. The theatre at that time played a vital part in religious ceremonies and celebrations where women were excluded and men played women's roles. The influence of Greece in this connection was so great that it was not until the sixteenth century that women appeared on the stage (Fig. 1).

These special features of the Greek stage demanded the use of masks, which the actor used during the performance and could change quickly.

1

FIG. 1. A Greek mask.

The Greek mask covered not only the actor's face but his head as well. He could change his appearance rapidly by taking off and putting on a different mask. It was therefore possible for three actors to play all the required parts. Each mask had a rigid expression appropriate to the interpreted character. It was a plastic image portraying the disposition, mood and temper of the character enabling the audience to recognize him immediately. The disadvantage of the mask, however, was the rigidity of its expression.

A characteristic feature of the mask was a wide opening at the mouth where a small mouthpiece was fixed to amplify the actor's voice so that he could be heard quite clearly in all parts of the vast amphitheatre.

The head of the actor covered with the mask and a wig as well was, of course, out of proportion to the rest of the body. To make up for this the actors used padded dresses and special shoes with thick soles and high heels.

The ancient Roman theatre differed in some aspects from that of Greece. The main difference was in the number of the actors. In the Roman theatre each actor had his own individual part to play. Masks were also used but they covered only the actors' faces. The masks also had wide apertures for the eyes and mouth and these enabled the actors to employ mime in their respective parts (Figs. 2 and 3).

The use of masks, however, never became a permanent feature because masks were quite inadequate to express all the emotions and gestures that acting required.

The most important trend in the history and development of make-up was the fact that the Etruscans who came to Rome as professional actors always played without masks. They emphasized the expression of the face by applying various pigments, vegetable juices, fats and powders.

Figs. 2 and 3. A Roman mask.

This was the basic change that profoundly influenced the impact of the actor's art and was, in fact, the origin of make-up as we know it today. Make-up has developed along with the technique of lighting and with the increasing demands upon the actor's appearance and performance required by the audience.

There was, however, a short return to the use of masks in Rome in the first century B.C. and then in the Middle Ages, especially in religious plays, and several centuries later in the Commedia dell'Arte. These revivals of masks were only temporary and short-lived.

When the open-air theatre was abandoned and plays were performed in buildings, in the houses of the nobility and later in theatres, it was necessary to illuminate the stage artificially. Torches and oil lamps, which had hitherto been used for this purpose, were replaced in the middle of the nineteenth century by gas light and finally by electric light.

The changes in the technical possibilities of the theatre have a direct influence on the technique of make-up as well. The better the stage is illuminated the finer and more natural the make-up of the actor must be. Natural appearance is gradually becoming more and more appreciated and preferred to the more rigid and sometimes death-like pallor due to heavy coats of grease paint.

The invention of the film had — and is still having — a tremendous influence on development of all parts of industry by its rapidly increasing technical needs.

At the outset the film observed all the traditions of the theatre. Later on the film adapted these traditions to its own use, gradually broke away from them and began creating new styles of its own. In some respects it has gone beyond the theatrical basis and has even begun to influence the theatre itself.

3

Make-up is one of the branches in which—especially in the last few years—the influence of the film upon the theatre has made itself felt.

Let us look back several decades to the beginning of the film. The only special requirements were the cine-camera and film negatives. Every other accessory was taken over from the theatre, for at that time no other techniques were known. Methods of directing, stage setting and lighting were drawn from the theatre and, of course, acting itself was greatly influenced by the theatre. Both the actor's performance and his make-up technique were that of the theatre. This was quite logical, for nothing more suitable for film work was known at that time. However, the first experience and the first results of film-making clearly showed that theatrical make-up was unsuitable for film purposes. It was necessary to solve problems unknown in the theatre, new ways had to be found, the differences between theatrical performance and the technique of film-making had to be levelled and new laws and rules resulting from certain specific properties of film negatives and character of lighting had to be considered and respected.

What are the principles and the purpose of modern make-up in film, television and theatre? First of all it must help the actor to look natural in the role he has to play. The make-up artist tries to use as little make-up as possible in modern film and television practice so as to emphasize the natural complexion. He concentrates his attention chiefly on the colour of the face. A realistic, natural performance is not in keeping with smooth faces covered with heavy layers of make-up, as were popular for so many years on the screen, but which looked artificial and lifeless.

The make-up man helps the actor to enhance the effect of his expression so that it looks natural and convincing to the audience watching the picture on the screen. The make-up man respects the natural pigmentation of the skin and tries to maintain a certain harmony in the make-up of all the players. The colour of the make-up differs only very slightly from that of the skin.

The most frequent type of make-up is that used for outlining or dramatizing a certain feature of the face, without actually changing the shape of the face or its parts. A rather more complicated task is the use of corrective make-up to narrow a broad jaw, to enlarge the eyes, to shorten a long face or to narrow a broad one, to straighten the bridge of the nose, etc., so that it corresponds to the current ideal of beauty. Every woman tries to achieve the same effect in her daily make-up.

The film negative often reacts to colour in quite a different way from the human eye. The illumination used in the studios may distort colours and natural appearance, and therefore any difference must be adjusted by the right type of make-up.

Make-up also helps to adjust the age of the actors when it does not correspond to that of the character represented in the part, because there is a tacit agreement that some types of roles require young performers.

The most complicated task for the make-up artist is to create a character which sometimes involves changes in the personality, basic features, nationality, race, age, etc. This can be done well only by an artist skilled as a craftsman and gifted with an inventive mind.

Recently more natural forms of make-up have been adopted by the theatre, the original source of film make-up. Just as with film in its early days, the theatre too is now making use of the latest principles of make-up for its own ends. The natural appearance of the actor is also highly important, but here again the distance between the stage and the audience must be considered and the make-up judged accordingly. Because of the distance factor, theatre make-up still remains somewhat more exaggerated but even so the make-up artists try to use as little make-up as possible choosing colour tones corresponding to those of the skin, and they portray the performers in the most natural way. Apart from make-up, greater care is devoted to wigs and hair accessories in the theatre nowadays.

In this way film, which in its infancy drew upon the theatre for its art and inspiration, is now able to repay its debt by rendering a like service to the theatre.

2. THE ANATOMY OF HEAD, ARMS AND HANDS

THE make-up artist cannot accomplish successfully any of the innumerable complicated tasks of his work without a basic knowledge of the anatomy of the human head. Without this knowledge he cannot venture to make any plastic changes of the face, so often required in character and corrective make-up. The sensitive lenses of the camera disclose wrongly accomplished corrective make-up or unnaturally looking plastic changes in the face and thus betray the dilletantism of the make-up man immediately. In addition, wrong make-up badly affects the actor's performance and can ruin his part.

The make-up artist must at least partly know the plastic anatomy or the anatomy of the external forms of the human body, describing their shape and proportions.

The external forms of the human body are given by the skeleton, the muscles and the skin with the subcutaneous connective tissue, containing a variable amount of fat in the adipose tissue.

The skeleton is the general framework of the body. It is built up mainly of a series of bones supplemented in certain regions by pieces of cartilage. Bones provide the central axis and give form to the body.

The muscles complete the body form. They possess the property of contractility, and movements of the body or of any of its parts are effected by the active contraction of a group or groups of voluntary muscles.

From the point of view of the make-up artist the most important muscles are the facial ones; they affect the expression of the face which reflects the external manifestations of the emotions of human beings.

The skin and the subcutaneous connective tissue with a variable amount of fat in the adipose tissue, complete fundamental forms of the body given by the skeleton and the muscles.

The external forms of the body are, however, considerably affected by the race and type, sex and age.

2.1. THE SKELETON OF THE HEAD—THE SKULL

The skull is the skeleton of the head. It is made up of a large number of bones which, with the exception of the mandible or lower jaw, are so

6

intimately connected to one another that no movement is possible between them. The skull consists of the egg-shaped *cranium* containing the brain and of the *facial skeleton* (Fig. 4).

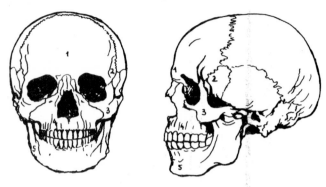

FIG. 4. The Skull. Left: anterior aspect; right: lateral aspect. 1. Frontal bone. 2. Temporal bone. 3. Zygomatic bone. 4. Maxillae. 5. Mandible.

The cranium is formed by the frontal bone, which passes backwards in the vault of the skull, where it meets the anterior borders of the right and left *parietal bones*, which together form the greater part of the top of the head. They extend backwards to meet the *occipital bone*, which forms the back of the head. Each parietal bone extends downwards on the side of the vault until it meets the upper limit of the *sphenoid bone* in front and the *temporal bone* behind.

The region of the forehead is formed by the frontal bone, which is usually convex. Two orbital plates project backwards from this bone and constitute most of the roof of the eye orbits. Sometimes the arches of the frontal bone framing the orbits are very obvious, especially in men's faces, and the line of the *nasal* bones to the forehead is very sharp. Such faces have a strict and determined expression. The line of the forehead to the nose in female and juvenile skulls is usually flatter and less obvious; the cranium of these skulls is also usually less vaulted than in the male skulls and the top of the female and juvenile skull is flatter. The female skull is smaller and very often more finely shaped but it is relatively broader than the male skull.

The ratio of the length to the breadth of the skull is also an important racial sign.

The *facial part* of the skull is much more important for the make-up man than the cranial part.

The facial part of the skull is composed of the *mandible* or the lower jaw, the *maxillae*, or the upper jaws. These bones form the upper boundary of the mouth and the lower and lateral boundaries of the anterior

7

nasal aperture. In addition, on each side the maxilla forms the medial part of the lower margin of the orbit, which completes the *zygomatic bone*. The frontal precesses of the two maxillae are separated from each other by the two *nasal bones*, which form the upper boundary of the anterior nasal aperture. The zygomatic bone is responsible for the prominence of the upper and anterior part of the cheek. It forms the lateral part of the lower margin of the orbital opening and ascends in the lateral margin to meet the frontal bone. The zygomatic process of the *temporal bone* passes forwards to meet the zygomatic or *cheek bone* and the two bones form the *zygomatic arch*.

The shape of the *orbit* considerably affects the features of the face. The orbits of babies are oval and very spacious, because the eyes of children are relatively very large, as the eyeballs hardly grow. The orbits of women appear more spacious than the orbits of men. The ratio of height to breadth of the eye orbit is important for the make-up artist, as it depends on the type of the face. Long and narrow faces have higher eye sockets, whereas the orbits in broad faces are low and broad.

The *anterior bony apertures of the nose* is pear-shaped and bounded by the nasal bones and the maxillae. A prominent, sharp projection marks the meeting of the two maxillae in the lower boundary of the aperture.

The shape of the nose cavity also depends on the type of the face as well as on the orbit. The shape of the nose is affected by the nasal bones. In women the root of the nose is usually broader than in men.

The *mouth* is formed by the maxillae and the *mandible*. The mandible is the largest and strongest bone of the face and has a curved, horizontal body which is arched, and two broad *rami* which project upwards from the posterior ends of the body. In the middle of the mandible is the *mental tubercle* or chin. In the upper and lower jaws are the teeth, which represent the support of the cheeks. In old age the bone is reduced in size. Following the loss of teeth, the alveolar part (the upper border of the body of the mandible) is absorbed, the ramus is oblique in direction, the angle measures about 140°, and the neck of the mandible is more or less bent back. The cheeks become hollow and the lips are sunken into the toothless mouth. The red colour of the lips is almost imperceptible and the mouth looks broader.

2.1.1. *Sex and Racial Differences in the Skull*

As a rule the skull of an adult female is lighter and smaller than that of the male. The muscular ridges are less marked, the superciliary arches and glabella are less prominent. The upper margin of the orbit is sharp, the forehead vertical, the frontal and parietal eminences prominent and the vault somewhat flattened. The contour of the face is rounder, the facial bones are smoother and the jaws and their teeth smaller.

Skulls vary in size and shape and the proportion of their length to breadth is an important racial sign. There are three types of skull shape: dolichocephalic — long and relatively narrow; mesaticephalic — the proportion of length to breadth is well balanced; brachycephalic — short and broad. Europeans are mostly mesaticephalitic, the skulls of the Nordic and the Mediterranean types being nearer to the dolichocephalitic shape than the Alpine and Eastern types, whose skulls are shorter and more like brahcycephalic. Prehistoric people were mostly dolichocephalitic, at present Kaffirs and native Australians represent the dolichocephalic types. Europeans and Chinese are mesaticephalic, and the Mongolians are brachycephalic.

2.2. THE MUSCLES

Muscular tissue forms the "fleshy" part of the body, and represents 45 per cent of the total body weight. Its main role, however, is to effect movements of the whole body or its parts. In order that a muscle may exercise its function of producing movements it must be attached at both of its extremities. When a muscle contracts, one of its attachments remains relatively stationary while the other is approximated to it. The term *origin* is used to designate the more fixed attachment and the term *insertion* to designate the movable point at which the force of the muscle is applied. As a general rule, so far as the limbs are concerned, the origin is the more proximal extremity of a muscle and the insertion the more distal.

The voluntary muscles are attached to the bones, cartilages, ligaments, skin or to other muscles, either directly or through the medium of fibrous structures called tendons and aponeuroses. Most muscles are provided with tendons at one or both extremities. Tendons or sinews are usually cord- or band-like in appearance. The individual fibres of the voluntary muscle are bound together into bundles or fasciculi by a connective tissue covering. The contraction of the muscle which causes movements changes the shape of the muscle. Facial muscles are very interesting for the make-up artist.

2.2.1. *The Facial Muscles and their Activity*

The fibres of the muscles of facial expression are inserted into the skin. The most important muscles affecting the expression of the face are the following:

The chewing muscles or masseters set the lower jaw into motion. The superficial portion of the chewing muscle is quadrilateral in shape and arises by a thick aponeurosis from the zygomatic process of the maxilla. Its fibres pass downwards and backwards to be inserted into the angle of the ramus of the mandible. The chewing muscles become very apparent while masticating, especially in the faces of thin people. When the muscles are contracted the teeth are firmly set. They are very important for expressing anger (Fig. 5).

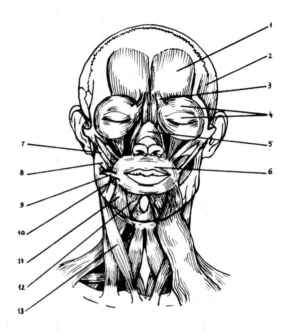

FIG. 5. The main facial muscles, namely the muscles of facial expression. 1. Frontal bellies. 2. Temporal muscle. 3. Corrugator. 4. Orbicularis oculi muscle. 5. Nasal muscle. 6. Orbicularis oris muscle. 7. Major zygomatic muscle. 8. Chewing muscle. 9. Risorius muscle (the muscle of smile). 10. Buccinator. 11. Triangular muscle of the mouth. 12. Quadrilateral muscle of the lower lip. 13. Sternomastoid muscle.

The temporal muscle is a fan-shaped muscle situated at the side of the head. It arises from the whole of the temporal fossa. The temporal muscle elevates the mandible and so closes the mouth. When the mouth is opened the temporal muscle is extended and does not fill the temporal fossa which then becomes obvious. The fossa seems deeper when the zygomatic bone is more arched, for example in the faces of people of the yellow race, or when a person gets thinner.

The muscles of the eyelids are a group of muscles, the most important of them being the orbicularis oculi. It is a broad, flat elliptical muscle which occupies the eyelids, surrounds the circumference of the orbit, spreads over the temporal region and downwards on the cheek. It consists of the orbital and palpebral portions. The palpebral portion acts involuntarily, closing the lids gently, as in sleep or in blinking. The orbital portion is subject to will. When the entire muscle is brought into action, the skin of the forehead, temple and cheek is drawn towards the medial angle of the orbit and the eyelids are firmly closed. The skin thus drawn is thrown into folds, especially radiating from the lateral angle of the eyelids. These folds become permanent in old age and form the so-called "crow's feet".

The frontal is the muscle of the forehead. It has no bony attachments. Acting from above, the frontal bellies raise the eyebrows and the skin over the root of the nose; acting from below they draw the scalp forwards, throwing the skin of the forehead into transverse wrinkles. In the ordinary action of the frontal bellies the eyebrows are elevated, thus giving the expression of surprise to the face. If the action is exaggerated the eyebrows are raised still further and the skin of the forehead thrown into transverse wrinkles as in the expression of fright or horror.

The muscles of the nose are represented by four muscles. The most important is the *procerus*, a small pyramidal slip continuous with the medial part of the frontal bellies of the forehead. It arises from the fascia covering the lower part of the nasal bone and the upper part of the upper nasal cartilage. The procerus draws down the medial angle of the eyebrow and produces the transverse wrinkles over the bridge of the nose.

The muscles of the mouth play an important part in the expression of the face. The muscle surrounding the mouth is called the orbicularis oris, the sphincter muscle of the mouth. It is made up of several layers of fibres surrounding the mouth orifice but having different directions. In its normal action this muscle effects the direct closure of the lips. By its deep fibres, assisted by oblique ones, it compresses the lips against the teeth. The superficial part of this muscle brings the lips together and protrudes them.

The buccinator is a thin quadrilateral muscle, occupying the space between the maxilla and the mandible. It compresses the cheeks against the teeth so that during the process of mastication the food is kept under the immediate pressure of the teeth. When the cheeks are distended with air the buccinators expel it between the lips as in blowing a trumpet.

The major zygomatic muscle arises from the zygomatic bone and is inserted into the angle of the mouth. It draws the corners of the mouth upwards and laterally, as in laughing.

The quadrilateral muscle of the upper lip is divided into three portions, or heads: the zygomatic head arising from the zygomatic bone; the central, infraorbital head, arising from the lower margin of the orbital opening; and the angular head, which arises from the upper part of the maxilla, passes obliquely downwards and is inserted into the lower nasal cartilage and skin of the nose. All three heads are inserted into

11

the muscular substance of the upper lip. This complex muscle raises and everts the upper lip, dilates the nostril and forms the nasolabial furrow, which passes from the side of the nose to the upper lip and gives an expression of sadness to the face. When the three heads of the muscle are in action together they give the expression of contempt to the countenance.

The nasolabial furrow markedly affects many expressions of the face. It is effected by the above-mentioned muscle and its contractions can either deepen or smooth the nasolabial furrow and produce the expressions of laughing or weeping.

The quadrilateral muscle of the lower lip arises from the oblique line of the mandible and passes upwards to be inserted into the skin of the lower lip. It draws the lip downwards and a little laterally, as in the expression of irony.

The triangular muscle of the lower lip arises from the oblique line of the mandible and its fibres are inserted by a narrow fasciculus into the angle of the mouth. It draws the corners of the mouth downwards giving a sad expression to the face.

The mental muscle is a conical fasciculus situated at the side of the frenulum of the lower lip. It arises from the mandible and is inserted into the skin of the chin. It raises and protrudes the lower lip and wrinkles the skin of the chin, expressing doubt or disdain.

The muscles of facial expression are always in pairs, except for the orbicularis oris. Each of them can either contract individually, or all of them can be brought into action together: the contractions can be either identical in both halves of the face or they can differ. The facial muscles can thus produce innumerable expressions and express many emotions.

Some emotional strains such as joy, anger, pain or fear, can cause involuntary contractions of the facial voluntary muscles and the resulting expression reflects the respective emotion. Children do not suppress these contractions of the facial muscles and it is easy to read their emotions in their faces. Adults, however, usually try to counteract the involuntary contractions and it is therefore very hard to learn their emotions by the expression of their faces. An actor has to master the expression of the face very well, so that he can express a required emotion in his performance no matter what he really feels personally.

2.3. THE SKIN

The skin covers the body and protects the deeper tissues. It plays an important part in the regulation of the body temperature and possesses limited excretory and absorbing powers.

For the make-up artist, however, skin is the most important component of the human head, because it represents the field of his own activity, upon which most of his attention is concentrated. He must, therefore, know the anatomy and properties of skin very well.

The skin consists of two principal layers — of a layer of vascular connective tissue, named the *dermis* and of an external covering called the *epidermis*.

The epidermis is non-vascular and consists of stratified epithelium. The uppermost layer is called the horny layer and is composed of horny cells, which gradually peel off and are replaced by other horny cells supplied from the lower layers. The cells containing pigment are in these lower layers. The *dermis* which is situated under the epidermis is tough, flexible and highly elastic. It contains numerous blood vessels which, together with pigment, give colour to the skin.

The complexion colour of the skin is due to two factors — the presence of *pigment* in the cells of the epidermis and to *haemoglobin*, the red pigment of the blood.

Sun and warmth increase the development of the dark pigment in the epidermis. The dark pigment protects against the harmful effects of the sun's rays and therefore the inhabitants of the equatorial countries have a very dark, sometimes almost black, complexion. The exposed parts of the body of white people also acquire a tawny colour, especially in the summer. The amount of pigment is not uniform on all the parts of the body.

2.3.1. *Transparency of Skin*

The degree of transparency of the skin depends on its thickness. In places where the skin is thick, as for instance on the palms of the hands and on the soles of the feet, the red blood pigment and the dark pigment of the epidermis cannot be observed and these respective parts of the body have the same colour in a white man as well as in a negro.

2.3.2. *Colour of the Skin*

The red blood pigment — haemoglobin — is the co-factor of the pigment in skin colouring. The red tone of the skin in parts of the body is due to the amount, the type and the lumen of the blood vessels in the corium. Some areas of the body, such as the lips, are coloured red, because the mucous membrane of the lips is very thin and the number of blood vessels in it is great, whereas other areas, the nipples for instance, are brownish, because the prevailing colour is that of the pigment. The colour of the skin can also be affected by certain external factors, such as the sun, as already mentioned, by heat and cold, by friction, by emotional strain like anger or shame, etc. All these factors, except the sun, affect the blood vessels, which dilate and the increased amount of blood tints the skin red. Venous blood gives a bluish tint to the skin, whereas arterial blood produces a vivid red tone.

The transparency of the skin plays an important part in its colouring. When the skin is highly transparent the colour of the skin is pinkish and generally lighter. For instance, the skin of children, young girls and women is lighter than the skin of men. In old age the skin loses its transparency, and the skin of old people is yellowish.

The amount of fat in the adipose tissue in the corium also affects transparency of the skin.

2.3.3. *Wrinkles and Furrows*

The character of the skin depends on the amount of fat in the adipose tissue in the corium, and on the way in which the skin is joined to its base. In some places the ridges and furrows are permanent and do not change with age. Most of the wrinkles and lines, however, are temporary in young age and deepen with advancing age, because the skin loses its elasticity, the amount of fat usually decreases and the skin remains lined.

The skin on the back of the hands is smoother in old age than in youth, because the skin grows thinner there and the tiny wrinkles are smoothed. The skin of the hands of old people is smooth, thin and shiny.

The *adipose tissue* is situated in the corium. The amount of fat in this tissue differs in different parts of the body; in some parts it is missing altogether, for instance on the eyelids, in the ear lobes and on the tip of the nose. The skin is fixed firmly to the base in these respective places and does not form wrinkles. In some places, however, the fat forms pads, as for instance, on the cheeks.

2.4. TYPES OF FACES

Faces can be divided into seven basic types (Fig. 6) according to their shapes.

1. *Oval* is an ideal shape of a face. The forehead is slightly broader than the chin.

2. *Round*: the typical marks are full cheeks and rounded jaws, very often a rounded hairline.

3. *Square*: the face is short with a straight hair line. The cheeks are not rounded and the general impression is angular.

4. *Oblong*: a long angular narrow face with a long nose.

5. *Triangular*: the forehead is broad, eyes set widely apart, narrow jaws and high cheek-bones. The hairline is irregular.

6. *Upturned triangle*: irregular hairline, broad mandible, narrow cheek-bones and deep set eyes.

7. *Rhomboid*: narrow forehead, high and very prominent cheek-bones and a narrow receding chin.

FIG. 6. Types of faces. 1, Oval. 2, Round. 3, Square. 4, Oblong. 5, Triangular. 6, Upturned triangle. 7, Rhomboid.

2.5. INDIVIDUAL PARTS OF THE FACE

This section describes the respective parts of the face, their function and the changes they undergo in ageing.

2.5.1. *The Eyes*

The eyes and their vicinity are the most important features of the upper part of the face. Their expression changes strongly with various emotions. The make-up artist must know what effects he can achieve by make-up and how the eyes affect the expression of the entire face.

The eye is set in the orbital cavity and only its front part is visible. The eyeball is round and a system of ocular muscles effects its movement. This is very important for various expressions of the face.

The outer fibrous coat of the eyeball is the sclerotic or the white of the eye. The sclerotic is transparent in the eyes of small children and the blood vessels in the deeper coats of the eye give the sclerotic a bluish tint. In old age, however, minute droplets of fat deposit in the sclerotic and give it a yellow tint (Fig. 7).

In front of the eyeball is the colourless and transparent cornea. When

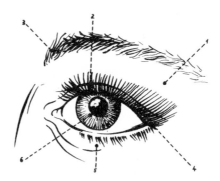

Fig. 7. The eye and its parts. 1. Upper eyelid ridge. 2. Eyelid. 3. Eyebrows. 4. Eyelashes. 5. Lower eyelid ridge. 6. Pupil.

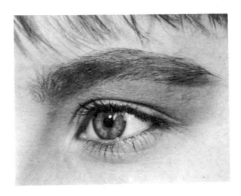

Fig. 7a. The eye.

the eyes are shut the cornea gives a slight curve to the eyelid. The cornea is moistened with the tears and it strongly reflects light.

The coloured iris is seen through the transparent cornea. The colour of the iris depends on the amount of pigment deposited in it. Clear blue eyes of newly born babies gradually darken when the pigment sets in the iris.

The colour of the eyes usually corresponds with the pigmentation of the skin and the hair, and depends on the race. The light-haired nordic types in northern Europe usually have blue eyes, whereas in the Mediterranean countries, dark hair and dark eyes are more common. However, dark-haired people often have blue eyes and light-haired people have dark eyes. Blue, grey, green, brown and black are the basic colours of the eyes.

2.5.1.1. *The position of the eyes.* The position of the eye is extremely important for the expression of the face. The eyes can be either deep-set or protruding, according to the amount of fat in the orbits, in which the eyeballs are imbedded.

Anger and alcohol dilate the blood vessels in the adipose tissue of the orbits, it increases its volume and the eyes protrude in consequence.

In old age or when the amount of fat in the orbit decreases (illness, worry, fatigue, etc.) the eyes are deep set. As a rule, dark circles appear under the eyes, because the transparency of the lower eyelid is also greater and the network of tiny blood vessels gives a blue tint to the area under the eyes.

Deeply set eyes appear smaller than they really are, because the super-ciliary arches are very prominent. Slightly protruding eyes have a happy and sincere expression which can be seen especially in the faces of children. Their eyes are too big in proportion to their face. The distance between the eyes is often an important feature of the face. It depends on the breadth of the root of the nose.

2.5.1.2. *Accessory structures of the eyes.* The accessory organs of the eye, most important for a make-up man, are the eyebrows and the eyelids. They protect the eyes from possible external injury. The upper eyelid is always bigger than the lower one. The shape and movement of the eyelids strongly affect the appearance of the entire eye area and of the eyes themselves.

The skin of the eyelids is very thin and slightly darker than the rest of the face. In the course of the years, especially in old age, wrinkles and furrows appear around the eyes. The orbital ridges running below the super-ciliary arches and the eyelid furrows that are in the centre of the upper eyelids change their shape with the passing years. This fact is especially important in character make-up. The orbital ridges are deeper in thin faces than in fat ones and are missing completely in the so-called Mongolian eye. The upper eyelids in this type of eye seem to be slightly swollen.

17

In older age the skin of the superciliary arches becomes limp and hangs over the orbital ridge as a skin fold. The limp skin of the lower eyelid forms bags under the eyes (Fig. 8).

FIG. 8. Mongolian eye. The skin fold of the upper eyelid partly covers the inner angle of the eye.

The upper orbital ridge is deepest near the inner corner of the eye, whereas in the outer corner it is almost imperceptible. The lower orbital ridge is shallow, starts in the inner angle of eye and passes to the cheek.

The eyelid furrows depend on the anatomy and function of the eyelids. The lower eyelid furrow is again shallow, the upper one is usually deep and parallel with the edge of the eyelid. In the eyes of the eastern races, the furrow is very near the line of the eyelashes.

The inner corner of the Mongolian eye is usually covered by a skin fold of the upper eyelid. This fold makes the eye appear more slanting than it really is. The edges of the eyelids converge in the inner and outer angle of the eye and thus form the eye aperture. The edges of the eyelids are relatively thick, usually pinkish and moist. Two or three rows of eyelashes grow in them. The lashes of the upper eyelids are long curved upwards, whereas the lashes of the lower eyelids are short and curved downwards. The inner angle of the eye is rather more marked than the outer one and a small protrusion can be observed there, called the *caruncula*.

Around the age of 30 years a number of tiny lines appears in the outer angle of the eyes. They are caused by the contractions of the circular eye muscle (the orbicularis oculis) and they disappear when the muscle is extended. In middle age these wrinkles remain permanent and are the first signs of ageing.

The orbit is framed with an eminence of skin which supports many short, thick hairs directed obliquely on the surface—the eyebrows. Sometimes they curve slightly upwards at the temple. The colour of the eyebrows is usually identical with that of the hair. Men's eyebrows sometimes join at the root of the nose and such faces have hard and determined expressions.

2.5.2. *The Nose*

The nose forms a three-sided pyramidal protrusion in the centre of the face. The nose is a very prominent feature of the face. It dominates the expression of the face and any irregularity, however small, strongly affects the features. The make-up man has to change the shape of the nose very often. He can narrow, broaden, bend or straighten the nose with skilfully applied make-up.

The shape of the nose is given by the skeleton of the head. The upper third of the nose is formed by two nasal bones, the remaining part is formed by the nasal cartilage(Fig. 9).

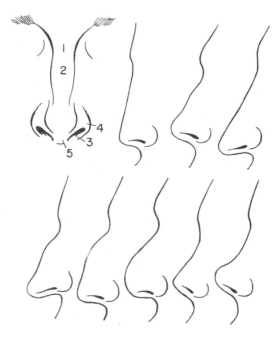

FIG. 9. Various shapes of nose. The first diagram shows the individual parts of the nose. 1. The root. 2. The bridge. 3. The nasal aperture. 4. The nostril. 5. The septum.

The septum of the nose is formed by a cartilage which divides the nasal cavity into two parts. The septum also affects the shape of the nose; a broad septum broadens the bridge of the nose.

The shape of the tip of the nose and of the nostrils is given by the shape of the lower basal cartilage and of the small cartilages of the nostrils. The upper end of the cartilages of the nostrils is outlined by gentle lines which change into the deep nasolabial furrows, the most obvious ridges in the face (Fig. 10).

The skin on the bridge of the nose is thin and contains a small amount

19

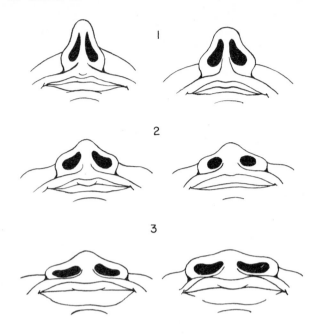

FIG. 10. Different shapes of nostrils. 1. White race. 2. Yellow race. 3. Negroes.

of subcutaneous tissue and is easily wrinkled. The skin on the tip of the nose and on the nostrils is thick and forms no wrinkles.

The individual parts of the nose, i.e. the bridge, the root and the tip as well as the pass to the forehead greatly affect the shape of the nose. Different shapes of noses are typical of different races.

The root of the nose lies between the inner angles of the eyes and its shape depends on the pass of the nose to the forehead. The so-called Greek nose has a high root and bridge, so that the pass to the forehead is almost imperceptible. Women more often than men have the imperceptible pass of the nose but the flat pass, typical for the Greek nose, is very rare. Men have curved noses more often than women.

Noses can be straight, curved, or concave with a great number of transient shapes and combinations. Short upturned noses are common among women and children. The curved nose is long and the tip is slightly bent down so that the nasal openings are not visible. The cartilage of the curved nose, however, is almost straight and only the bony part is bent. The Jewish nose has the cartilage curved and the bony part is nearly straight.

White men usually have relatively narrow and prominent noses. Their nostrils are narrow and their long axis points forward. The nostrils of the

20

yellow race are usually round and the nose is not too prominent. The negroes have very flat and broad noses, so that the nostrils are almost parallel with the upper lip.

2.5.3. The Lips

The lips are the most marked feature of the lower part of the face. They are set between the nose and the chin. They are formed only of muscles, the activity of which changes the shape of the lips and the size of the mouth aperture.

The lips are supported by the arches of the maxillae and of the mandible, with the teeth. In old age, when the teeth are missing, the lips sink in the mouth so that the red mucous membrane disappears, and the shape of the mouth changes into a straight line. Negroes have very prominent protruding lips, because they have much stronger obliquely growing teeth than other races. Women usually have fuller lips than men (Fig. 11).

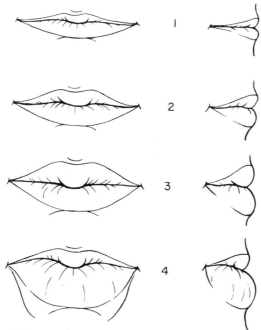

FIG. 11. The Lips: anterior and lateral aspects. 1. Thin lips 2. Medium-full lips. 3. Full lips. 4. Protruding lips.

The upper lip consists of a central, slightly depressed part, called the philtrum and of two side parts. The depression forms a little triangle and thus the heart-shaped line of the upper lip. The red mucous membrane of the upper lip curves upwards forming an arch from the outer angles of the mouth, joins the heart-shaped line in the middle of the mouth and thus

21

completes the beautiful soft line of the upper lip. The shape of the upper lip is sometimes changed with lipstick, as it is very important for a nice smile. The make-up man must make up the lips very carefully so as not to distort their proportion and shape. In day make-up the shape of the lips often changes according to fashion.

The side parts of the lips of men are covered with beard; on the upper lips of women and children there grow very soft and fine hairs.

The lower lip is usually a little receding. Both the upper as well as the lower lip are widest in the middle and narrow towards the corners.

2.6. THE SUBCUTANEOUS VEINS

The subcutaneous veins significantly complete the features of the head and hands. The position of the veins at the back of the hand is individual and characteristic for each person. Heat and physical strain increase the amount of blood in the veins and they are strongly marked.

The make-up artist must know the most important subcutaneous veins of the head, arms and hands.

2.6.1. *The Veins of the Face*
The frontal vein is in the centre of the forehead. It is a very strong and prominent vein which forms a Y near the inner corners of the eyes. Anger increases the amount of blood in this vein, it swells and becomes very obvious. Sometimes it is also called the vein of anger. The frontal

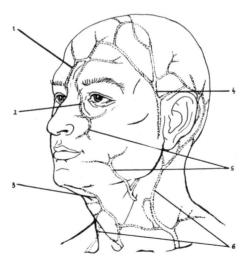

FIG. 12. The Superficial Veins of the Face and Throat. 1. The frontal vein. 2. The vein of the corner of the eye. 3. The anterior jugular vein. 4. The temporal vein. 5. The facial vein. 6. The external jugular vein.

22

vein passes downwards to the eye, there being called the vein of the corner of the eye, and down to the cheek, where it is called the facial vein.

The other of the most marked veins of the face is the *temporal vein*, which draws the blood off the hairy part of the head. This vein has a very complicated network of tributaries, which can be seen clearly in the upper part of the temporal and frontal area, whereas on the top of the head and on the nape it is only very faintly visible on bald heads.

The *temporal artery* follows the same route as the temporal vein. The artery forms one branch in the centre of the hairy part of the head and a second branch in the skin of the top of the head. The route of the artery itself and of both its branches is twisting and is particularly marked under the thin skin of older people (Fig. 12).

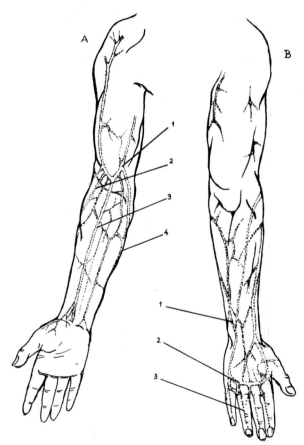

FIG. 13. The superficial veins of the arm and hand.
A. The palmar side of the arm and hand. 1. The median cubital vein. 2. The cephalic vein. 3. The median ante-brachial vein. 4. The basilic vein.
B. The dorsal side of the hand. 1. The basilic vein. 2. The dorsal metacarpal venous network. 3. The super dorsal veins of the fingers.

2.6.2. *The Subcutaneous Veins of the Neck*

The *jugular* vein runs on the outer side of the neck. It is very visible as the skin at the side of the neck is rather thin. The jugular vein is very obvious when singing, shouting, and when under physical strain.

2.6.3. *The Subcutaneous Veins of the Arm*

The superficial veins of the palm of the hand and the palm side of the fingers are very narrow so that they are not apparent. The veins of the back of the hand where the skin is very thin are very distinct because there is very little subcutaneous tissue.

The network of the blood vessels starts on the tips of the fingers where two stronger veins are formed from the network of the minute ones and they pass backwards at the back of the fingers. At the base of the fingers, two veins of the neighbouring fingers are joined together by oblique communicating branches. Those from the adjacent sides of the fingers unite to form three dorsal metacarpal veins, which end in a dorsal venous network. The radial part (on the thumb side of the hand) of the network is joined by the dorsal digital vein from the index finger and by the dorsal digital veins of the thumb, and is prolonged upwards as the *cephalic* vein. The ulnar part of the network (the little finger side of the hand) receives the dorsal digital vein of the little finger and is continued upwards as the *basilic vein.*

These two veins are the most obvious veins of the arm and sometimes they must be enhanced in character make-up (Fig. 13).

The other parts of the body are not important for the make-up man and are not mentioned in this chapter.

3. MAKE-UP AND LIGHT

LIGHTING is one of many factors that vitally affect the results of film or stage make-up.

In film and television studios, as well as on the stage, only artificial light is used. Out-of-doors, the sun is usually the main source of light, sometimes combined with other auxiliary sources of artificial light. No light source, however, is neutral as far as colour is concerned and the quality — or colour temperature — of the source greatly affects the colours of the actor's face. It is most important for the make-up artist to know which colour will be absorbed and which will become more apparent in the particular light used. He must therefore possess a good basic knowledge of light and colours so as to create a perfect mask; to supervise and maintain the right colour of the make-up in different stage settings and built-up scenes, when different lighting and filters are necessary during the performance.

The make-up artist must also know the sensitivity of various film emulsions to different colours and the colour changes obtained by the use of different filters.

This chapter is intended to help the make-up artist to get rapidly familiar with the basic factors that may affect the colour of the make-up.

3.1. ILLUMINATION

Lighting is — in the technical sense of the word — the amount of light necessary to illuminate the scene, the actors and the props in the studio, on the stage or out-of-doors, having regard to the speed and quality of the negative.

In the artistic sense, lighting is a factor which considerably affects the atmosphere and artistic impact of the scenery. Close co-operation between the make-up artist and the cameraman is absolutely necessary. Correct lighting helps the make-up artist to bring out all the finesse of his art while faulty illumination can mar the effects of make-up completely. The cameraman usually prefers to regard the composition of the scene as a whole but certain shots require his attention to be focused solely on the expression of the actor's face; at that point the make-up man has to consider most carefully the quality of light in relation to the colour scheme of the applied make-up.

25

3.2. LIGHT AND COLOUR

The colour of every object as seen by the human eye is defined by the quality of the incident light and by the amount of reflected and absorbed light. Any object can reflect or absorb daylight either partly or completely. If the object reflects the total amount of incident light, the human eye sees it as colourless, whereas if it absorbs the light completely it appears black. Objects that absorb only a certain part of the incident light of a certain wavelength and reflect all others, are coloured.

If, for example, an object absorbs red rays, the reflected rays give it a blue–green colour and vice versa; an object absorbing yellow rays looks blue. When the absorbed and reflected rays mix, the resulting impression is white. The absorbed and reflected rays complement each other in achromatic light and are called complementary rays. If an object absorbs and reflects all types of rays equally it acquires a grey colour, the intensity of which grows with increasing absorption.

3.3. LIGHT DIFFRACTION

Achromatic light disintegrates in a glass prism yielding the following colour bands: red, orange, yellow, green and violet, which form the spectrum. This diffraction is caused by different refractory indexes of the individual rays, i.e. they diverge more if they are violet rays and less if they are red, from the straight line in which the white light has entered the prism. Daylight also contains ultraviolet and infrared radiations which are not visible to the human eye. The colours differ in the wavelength of their radiations. The wavelength is expressed either in nanometres or Ångströms, 1 nm being 10 Å. Visible radiation extends from approximately 400 nm at the blue end of the spectrum to approximately 700 nm at the red end. The infrared region continues beyond this wavelength towards higher values, whereas the ultraviolet region covers the range between 250–400 nm. The visible part of the spectrum is a small fraction of the complete light spectrum of the sun.

If an object absorbs light in the ultraviolet region, it is colourless to the human eye. If it absorbs violet or blue rays it is yellow. When the absorption takes place in the green region, the object is orange or red and the absorption in the red region gives the object a blue or green colour. An optical colour impression may thus be achieved by mixing the absorbed and transmitted light components.

The colour depends on the absorption of the radiations of different wavelengths. This fact explains why two pigments of different colours mixed together do not give the same colour as when the light of wavelengths corresponding to the colours of the pigments is mixed. For example, when yellow and blue radiations mix, the resulting colour is white, whereas the mixture of yellow and blue pigments is green. Yellow pigment absorbs blue and violet rays and blue pigment absorbs red and yellow rays. The mixture of these two pigments absorbs radiation of all wavelengths except green ones which are reflected. They enter the eye and the mixture is seen as green.

Table 1 shows the relation between wavelength and colour.

TABLE 1. *Wavelength and colour*

Wavelength (nm)	Colour
250–400	Ultraviolet
400–425	Violet
425–455	Indigo
455–475	Blue
475–510	Blue–green
510–565	Yellow–green
565–590	Yellow
590–620	Orange
620–650	Light red
650–750	Dark red
750–1500	Infra red

The principal colours (of pigments) are red, blue and yellow. Mixed together in equal parts they yield a grey colour. Secondary colours — orange, green and violet — result from mixing red and yellow, yellow and blue and red and blue, i.e. two of the principal colours. The complementary colours correspond to the principal ones as follows: yellow to violet, red to green, blue to orange. Various colour shades may be obtained by blending pigments of different colours either in equal parts or in suitable proportions. If blue prevails in a mixture of green and blue, the resulting tint is blue–green. If, on the contrary, more green is added, the shade is green–blue.

The principal colours of light are red, green and blue. If they are mixed in equal parts, the resulting light is white. Any required colour may be obtained by using suitable filters.

3.4. COLOURS AND THE HUMAN EYE

What happens in the eye and why do we see colours? According to our present — still rather incomplete — knowledge, we suppose that three different systems of perception most probably exist in the eye. Each system reacts separately to one-third of the light spectrum and causes the irritation of the particular optical nerves.

The process of sight is approximately as follows: the lens of the eye projects the image of an object on the retina which is composed of very fine cells, arranged as a mosaic, and these are the centre of perception. There are two types of cells — rods and cones. The former are very sensitive and react even in very dim light, but their colour perception is very poor: in dim light therefore we cannot distinguish colours properly and see only grey shades. The cones react only in bright light and are very sensitive to colours.

Objects do not usually absorb or transmit light in a uniform way. Daylight, which contains all the wavelengths, is usually partly absorbed, partly transmitted and partly reflected by surrounding objects. The existence of the many colour shades that can be seen in nature is due to this fact.

We distinguish the colour of light emitted by a light source from that of an object, for the latter is really light reflected by the particular object.

It is very important to bear this in mind, because lighting vitally affects the make-up in any film or stage set. It is therefore neccessary to distinguish the difference between the colour of light and the colour of make-up. The coloured tones of light do not always correspond to the colours of make-up. The dependence of the colours of make-up on light is most marked on the stage. Red tones in the make-up disappear under a red light, whereas in green light red in the make-up looks black. This fact may be used to obtain certain light effects (see Chapter 7). The correct combination of light and make-up emphasizes the efforts of the make-up artist and the effect of his work.

3.5. LIGHT SOURCES

The original source of light was the sun. At first, theatres were outdoors; later, when plays were performed in buildings, artificial sources of light were used, such as torches, candles, oil lamps and gas illumination. Neither of these sources, however, had any device for the correct focusing of light. Regulating and directing of light, and its character, was not obtained until the introduction of electric light which rapidly replaced all other inadequate sources.

The first film studios used daylight and the sun as the main source of light, and had glass or sliding roofs. Light used to be focused by various kinds of reflectors.

At present two types of light sources are used — strong bulbs and arc lighting. Photofloods are used on the stage as well as in film and television studios. Arclights are used only in film studios and sometimes even for outdoor shots.

3.6. TYPES OF LIGHTING

The make-up artist should know beforehand the kind of lighting which will be used, as the appearance of the same make-up differs in arclight and in light supplied by a small reading-lamp.

3.6.1. *Film Studio Lighting*

The total illumination of the scene is composed of key and direction lighting. Key lighting illuminates the complete scene with the essential amount of light. It is usually dispersed and does not cast any shadows. The direction lighting stresses the most important features of the scene and may be used as main lighting.

Key light is the determining factor of the exposure times and illuminates the most important parts of the scenery.

Booster light decreases the contrasts of the illumination and lightens the deep shadows.

Modelling light, or contour light, illuminates the set-up from the rear or from above. It helps to give the picture greater depth.

Background light is used when a high amount of light is required or if the background is important.

Effect light is used to achieve various effects as, for example, moonlight, daylight, street lighting, etc.

3.6.2. *Lighting in the Theatre*

"Cold" and "warm" lamps are mainly used for stage illumination. To achieve certain moods and effects such as early morning, sunrise, night, red sunset, dusk, etc., only one type of light is used or colour filters are placed in front of the lamps.

As the bulbs on the stage emit yellow light, the theatre make-up must have a slightly pinkish tone to make it look more natural.

Stage make-up should be almost identical with that used for colour film. The character of lighting is the only factor that may possibly have an unfavourable effect on the colours of the make-up on the stage and is usually allowed for beforehand. This situation is simpler than in the case of colour film, where many other factors may alter the final appearance of the make-up, such as the quality and character of negative emulsions and changes which the colours may undergo during the processing of the film. On the stage, red remains red and blue remains blue, except in situations where the make-up is changed by light effects, through the use of colour filters. There are no colour temperature problems on the stage, such as are all too common with colour film.

3.6.3. *Television Lighting*

Television lighting problems are rather different from those mentioned

29

above. The complete set-up is illuminated by the chief cameraman who decides the location of the light sources, controls the intensity and flow of light on his monitor in the control-room and thus prepares suitable illumination for all cameras used in the programme. Shots for a television programme are usually taken by three cameras placed at different angles and at different distances from the scene. Each is operated by its own cameraman who cannot choose the best illumination for his particular shot independently.

Television lights are mainly ceiling-mounted and illuminate the scene from above. Low light is used very rarely, chiefly in the "television theatre", i.e. in proper buildings adapted for television use. The upper light causes shadows under the eyebrows and eyes, and creates unwelcome highlights in the face which cannot easily be concealed.

The first camera tubes in the early days of television did not successfully reproduce the colours in their corresponding grey tones. The make-up man thus had to avoid certain colours and exaggerate others to make the monochromatic effect look more natural. The present image-orthicon tubes reproduce colours in grey tones almost as faithfully as panchromatic film.

The same general rule applies to television illumination as to film and stage lighting: it can either mar or enhance the effect of make-up. The only difference between film and television make-up is that the former is watched on a large film screen and the latter on a much smaller television screen.

3.7. COSTUMES, LIGHTING AND MAKE-UP

Make-up must be in perfect harmony with the whole appearance, i.e. in the first place with the costumes, their style and colour. The relationship among these factors is almost identical in film and television. Generally speaking, when soft lighting with pale background and pale dresses are used, the basic colour of the make-up should also be pale. Where costumes and dark background or more intense illumination is needed, darker make-up should be used.

Jewellery, bracelets, rings, etc., usually reflect light that is very difficult to control. White is also a very unhappy colour in television as the adjacent areas seem very dark. This is most marked when the actors are wearing white shirts and collars. White should be always replaced by pastel-coloured material. The problem caused by white colours in film is of minor importance as light control is much easier than in television.

An actor dressed in black is sometimes hardly distinguishable in a dark background, especially in television, because the colours, as in monochromatic film, show up as various tones of grey. Yellow and pale blue appear white and materials of these colours are used for shirts and blouses to avoid the use of white material. Light grey, green and brown appear a little darker and their shade depends on the intensity of the colour of the particular object. Royal or sky-blue looks grey, red and green are dark grey, and navy-blue appears very dark. Grey and brown provide various tones of grey from light to dark with more or less the same degree of intensity as the original colours. Ivory and beige are light grey.

In colour film it is advisable to avoid bright blue or bright red. They are too striking and affect the other colours. Very often they even distort the colours of the make-up which then looks unnatural. "Colour-scheme" tests of costumes, make-up, props and all the set-up should be carried out before the actual filming.

3.8. MAKE-UP AND FILM NEGATIVES

The majority of make-up problems are closely related to the character of the negative emulsions. The spectral sensitivity of the emulsions differs from that of the human eye, which itself is not uniformly sensitive to all colours. The greatest sensitivity of the eye lies within a narrow region around 550 nm, i.e. in the yellow spectral band. The sensitivity to colours decreases in both directions towards the red as well as towards the blue regions. To eliminate colour distortion, the negative emulsion should be approximately of the same sensitivity to colours as the human eye. The monochromatic film should reproduce colours of equal tones depths in about the same tones of grey, and the colours reproduced by the colour film should be as faithful as possible. The situation is, however, somewhat different in practice.

The original emulsions used to be only sensitive to a blue spectral band and all other colours were unsuitably reproduced in grey tones. The colour distortion was very strong because red, green and yellow all appeared uniformly dark. Orthochromatic emulsions which were used later were not much better. They were very sensitive to blue, less to green and not at all to red. Red appeared very dark and blue very light. Panchromatic emulsions are least sensitive to green. Their sensitivity to blue is about half of that to red, which does not differ very much from the colour sensitivity of the eye.

The emulsions used at present are usually orthopanchromatic. They are much more sensitive to colours and reproduce them much more faithfully. This fact is most important for the make-up as the make-up man can easily be guided by the colour sensitivity of the eye. The result of his work does not actually differ from the image thrown onto the screen.

31

3.9. THE SPEED OF FILM NEGATIVES

Films are either monochromatic or colour. Monochromes reproduce colours as a scale of grey shades, whereas the colour films reproduce the original colours more or less faithfully.

The most widely used negatives for studio shots at present are those of 20 DIN speed. For outdoor filming the speed may be a little lower. High speed films, such as Eastman Tri-X Type 5233, 27 DIN are rarely used as they usually have coarse grain. The following, however, are quite common: Eastman Plus-X Type 4321, 21 DIN or Eastman Kodak Double-X, 24 DIN approximately, which are noted for their fine grain and high selectivity.

Films of suitable selectivity and fine grain made by Ferrania (Panchro C 8, 19 DIN; Panchro 30, 21 DIN; and Panchro S 4, 25 DIN) are widely used because of the favourable properties mentioned above.

The biggest film manufacturers focus their attention on producing high-speed emulsions. The present tests and experiments with ultra-sensitive films of 30 DIN show, however, that many problems arise with the size of grain and selectivity. In spite of these facts, the development of very fast films is by no means over. The situation is getting more and more complicated by the introduction of wide-angled films which demand extra high selectivity and fine grain.

The monochromatic emulsions may be divided into several groups according to their speed. Each of them is suitable for a particular range of filming. Tables 2–5 show the speed groups.

TABLE 2. *Slow-speed monochromatic negative films*

Film	Speed in		
	DIN	ASA	WESTEN
	day and artificial light		
Ferrania P-3	17/10, 16/10	40, 32	32, 24
Du Pont Type 904B Superior I	16/10		
Eastman USA Background X	18/10		
Gevaert Gevapan 27 Type 152	17/10, 15/10	32, 20	24, 16
Ilford Engl. Pan F	16/10		
Orwo Negative-Film NP 3	15/10	25	

The speed of these films ranges from 13 to 18 DIN. They are noted for extra fine grain. They are mainly used for outdoor shots in good light and for television films.

TABLE 3. *Medium-speed monochromatic negative films*

Film	Speed in		
	DIN	ASA	WESTEN
	day and artificial light		
Ferrania Panchro S 2	21/10, 20/10	100, 80	80, 64
Ferrania Panchro C 7	21/10, 20/10	100, 80	
Agfa Isopan ISS	21/10		
Ansco USA Supreme	19/10		
Eastman Plus X Panchromatic	21/10		
Du Pont USA Type 926 B Superior II	21/10		
Gevaert Gevapan 30 Type 164	21/10, 19/10	80, 50	64, 40
Ilford Engl. FP 3	21/10		
Orwo Negative-Film	22/10	125	

The speed ranges from 19 to 21 DIN. The grain is sufficiently fine and the films show normal contrast. They are suitable for studio and outdoor shots in normal light conditions. They are well balanced in speed and grain size.

TABLE 4. *Fast monochromatic negatives*

Film	Speed in		
	DIN	ASA	WESTEN
	day and artificial light		
Eastman Double X	24/10		
Ferrania Panchro S-4	25/10		
Gevaert Gevapan 33 Type 183	23/10, 22/10	125, 100	100, 80
Ilford Engl. HP 3	25		

These are fast films, suitable for studio shots with variable levels of light or when greater depth is needed without increasing the illumination.

TABLE 5. *Extra fast monochromatic negative films*

Film	Speed in		
	DIN	ASA	WESTEN
	day and artificial light		
Du Pont USA Type 928 Superior 4	27		
Eastman Tri-X Panchromatic	27		
Gevaert Gevapan 36 Type 191	26/10, 25/10	250, 200	200, 160
Ilford Engl. HPS	28		
Orwo Negative-Film NP 7	27/10	400	
Orwo Negative-Film NP 71	27/10	400	

Extrafast materials with sensitivity higher than 25 DIN are suitable for a wide range of shots when the level of light is low, for example, for shots in twilight, at dusk and at night, and for objects that are difficult to illuminate adequately. Reversal films are not used in professional filming and are not mentioned in this book.

3.10. FILTERS

To obtain various colour and light effects as, for example, daylight, dusk, red evening glow or sunlight and moonlight, coloured filters are used on the stage. Filters are either heat-resistant plastic sheets or glass slides. They are mounted in front of the source of light and transmit only that part of the light spectrum that corresponds to their colour, for example a red filter transmits only a red spectral band so that the resulting light is red. All other wavelengths are absorbed by the filter. Similar coloured filters are used in the film studios to obtain appropriate colour effects or to regulate the colour temperature of various light sources and film negatives.

The filters, of course, greatly affect the colours of make-up. The make-up man can, however, immediately judge the final effect on the illuminated scene and can adjust its tones if neccessary.

The dependence of make-up on the illumination is shown in Table 6.

TABLE 6. *Make-up and light*

Colour of make-up	Colour of light				
	Red	Yellow	Green	Blue	Violet
Red	Disappears	Red	Very dark	Dark	Light red
Orange	Light red	Disappears	Dark	Very dark	Light
Yellow	White	Disappears	Dark	Light violet	Pink
Green	Very dark	Dark grey	Light green	Light green	Blue
Blue	Dark grey	Grey	Dark green	Light blue	Dark violet
Violet	Dark blue	Blue	Dark blue	Violet	Light violet

However, a much more difficult situation arises when correction filters are used and mounted in front of the camera lenses. They correct certain properties of the negative, especially its sensitivity to colours and colour temperature. They also strongly affect the colours of the make-up. The make-up artist cannot immediately see the possible changes of the make-up colours and has to wait for the results of photographic tests. It is therefore very important for him to know the properties of the most frequently used correction filters, especially in relation to the particular character of lighting and negative emulsion.

If mixed lighting is used—bulbs and arcs—with different colour temperatures, filters are mounted in front of the arc-lights.

Filters help to correct the colour temperature of light illuminating the scene and convert the colour of the secondary light to that of the main light. The use of these filters is shown in Table 7.

TABLE 7. *Colour temperature conversion filters*

Main light	Secondary light	Colour temperature filters adjusting the colour of the secondary light
Daylight	M.R.H.I. Arc Spot M.R.Arc 40A Duarc Tungsten C.P. or M.P.	Brigham Y 1 or Ferrania CT 34 Macbeth Whiterlite
C.P. or M.P. Tungsten Light	M.R.H.I. Arc Spot M.R. Arc 40A Duarc	Brigham Y 1 + Y 2 or Ferrania CT 34 + CT 35
	Nitraphot or Photo- flood Lamps	Brigham Y 2 or Ferrania CT 33
M.R.H.I. Arc Spot + Brigham Y 1	C.P. or M.P. Tungsten Light	Macbeth Whiterlite

For some shots (high mountains, snow, sea) ultraviolet or haze filters must be used, to suppress any excess of blue present in colour film, and haziness in monochromatic film. Wratten 85 filter is suitable for colour temperature above 5800°K.

3.10.1. *Colour Filters for Monochromatic Films*

Colour filters used for monochromes transmit light and have a wavelength corresponding to their own colour. Other wavelengths are absorbed. These effects are indicated in Table 8.

TABLE 8. *Colour filters for monochromes*

Filter colour	Absorbs	Transmits
Red	Green and blue	Red
Green	Red and blue	Green
Blue	Green and red	Blue
Azure (cyan)	Red	Blue and green (cyan)
Magenta	Green	Red and blue (magenta)
Yellow	Blue	Green and red (yellow)

If a filter is used for filming an object of approximately the same colour as the filter, the reproduction appears lighter. Conversely, if the filter absorbs the particular colour, the object appears darker. The effect also largely depends on the type of emulsion. Panchromatic emulsions are used most often, but sometimes even orthochromatic ones with a yellow filter. A suitable filter is usually chosen experimentally by comparing several shots of the same object filmed through different filters. A safer way, however, is to carry out photographic tests, for the colour sensitivity of the human eye differs from the sensitivity of emulsions. The majority of panchromatic emulsions are very sensitive to blue and ultraviolet light, and therefore blue and violet objects seem very pale when reproduced and there is little contrast between white snow and a blue sky.

Some super-pan films, however, are highly sensitive to red, especially when used in tungsten light and the reproduced red objects appear very light.

Contrast filters correct the intensity of the monochromatic reproduction of some colours, and increase the clearness and contrast between colours that otherwise would be reproduced in grey tones that are almost identical.

Haze filters absorb ultraviolet light that usually shows as haziness in panorama shots filmed on a clear day. Atmospheric haze scatters almost no infrared radiations, very little red light, some green light, more blue light and a large amount of ultraviolet light. The majority of photographic emulsions are sensitive to blue and ultraviolet and unfiltered shots of distant landscapes will therefore show more marked haze than is visible to the human eye.

Neutral-density filters equally absorb all wavelengths of the visible spectrum range and reduce the amount of light reaching the film to the required level without any effect on its colour, for example while filming in strong sunshine. They also reduce the intensity of flashlights placed too near the subject being photographed, for instance in portrait photography. They can also be used in combination with other filters.

Tables 9 and 10 briefly outline the types and use of Kodak Wratten filters and Orwo–Wolfen filters.

TABLE 9. *Kodak Wratten filters*

Filter Wratten	Colour	Use
8	Yellow	Pan-films used in daylight
9	Medium yellow	Rendering blue sky
11	Light yellow–green	Pan-films in tungsten light
25	Red	Strong contrasts
29	Dark red	Selective filter for strong contrast effects
38	Pale blue	Contrast filter for pan-films.
80B	Pale blue	Corrects too pale reproduction of red in tungsten light
ND 01	Neutral-density grey filters	Reduce the amount of light to required levels
ND 02		
ND 03–09		
ND 1 0		
ND 2 0		

TABLE 10. *Orwo–Wolfen filters for monochromatic negative films*

Filter	Colour	Use
0–5	Yellow (gradual density)	Reduces blue and violet rays for daylight filming
70	Light green	For NP5 negative films, photofloods
72	Yellow–green	For NP3, NP5, NP7 negative films
80	Light red	Effect filter for NJ 750
81	Red	Effect filter for NJ 750
82	Dark red	Effect filter for NJ 750
91	Light grey	Neutral-density grey filters for reducing lighting
93	Grey	without any change in the shutter setting; suitable for daylight
95	Grey	
97	Grey	Neither of these filters can be used for Orwocolor

3.11. COLOUR NEGATIVE FILMS

The basic principle of all colour films in use at present is that the colours are separately, but simultaneously, recorded on the negative and then transferred to a single positive print. The colours are divided into three colour groups during filming and joined together in reproducing.

From our knowledge of the process of colour vision in the human eye, we can infer that the photographic colour picture is also a combination of three separate basic colour pictures.

There are two ways of obtaining a colour picture in the film emulsion. The first is based upon three emulsion layers, each of them being sensitive to one basic colour. The second method is based upon a combination of the light of three different colours. The former method is called the subtractive process (Technicolor system), the latter the additive colour synthesis.

The subtractive process needs the three colours which when combined, will yield the greatest number of pure colour shades, namely yellow, purple and blue–green. Each of these colours absorbs two-thirds and transmits one-third of the visible spectral region. In this subtractive process three separate colour pictures are formed. This is achieved by filters within the emulsion that transmit the remaining one-third of the spectral region, i.e. they are complementary to the colour of the particular picture. The separate colour pictures are called the blue filter shot or yellow extract, the green filter shot or purple extract and the red filter shot or blue–green (blue) extract. Three separate coloured pictures obtained by light diffraction are combined in the three emulsion layers of the film in the complementary colours of the filmed objects. The true colours are reproduced on the emulsion of the positive copy.

37

Colour negative films have three separate layers of emulsion, sensitive to one spectral region. Each of the emulsion layers subtracts one-third of the white light. These are the so-called multilayer films.

Table 11 shows the most frequently used colour film materials.

TABLE 11. *Colour film negatives and their speed*

Film	Speed in		
	DIN	ASA	WESTEN
Anscocolor Negative Type 845	18/10		
Eastmancolor Type 5250	18/10		
Orwocolor Negative-Film NC 1	16/10	32	
Gevacolor Negative Type 652	17/10	32	24
Ferraniacolor Negative Type 82	15/10	20	16
Ferraniacolor Negative Type 54	13/10	12	10

3.11.1. *Filters for Colour Films*

Filters for colour films are quite different from those used for monochromatic films, and these two types of filters cannot be interchanged.

Haze filters are also used to remove the blue tone which often appears on shots of distant landscapes, mountains, snow or large stretches of water such as the sea, big lakes, etc., caused by a lot of ultraviolet light present in the atmosphere. The resulting haze produces rather a cold impression which is often undesirable, like the haziness on monochromes caused in the same way.

The human eye is remarkably adaptable to the intensity and colour of the illumination. In varying conditions this automatic adjustment results in shifting the apparent colour of a given light source towards white. If, for example, we look at a sheet of white paper in tungsten light, we do not notice the yellow colour of the light. If, on the other hand, we switch on tungsten light in daytime when the eyes are already adapted to daylight, the yellow tone of the tungsten lamp immediately becomes very apparent.

However, the films are not adaptable to the colour quality of light and if an object is illuminated by tungsten light and filmed on a colour film for daylight the colours reproduced will be very distorted. If, therefore, a colour film is exposed to light of an unsuitable colour temperature a correction filter must be used. Generally, the colour film reproduces colours most faithfully when it is exposed to the light of the particular colour temperature for which the emulsion has been prepared and balanced. If a reel of film is to be exposed to artificial light as well as to daylight, it is advisable to use a suitable correction filter for daylight but for artificial lighting no filter is necessary.

Negative colour films for different kinds of artificial light may be used in daylight when suitable filters correct and adjust the colour temperature of daylight. These filters also correct the difference in the colour temperature of various sources of artificial light.

Table 12 presents a survey of filters for colour films.

TABLE 12. *Kodak Wratten filters for colour films*

Filter	Colour	Use
Ultraviolet Filter 1A	Pink	Eliminates the blue tone and haze caused by ultraviolet light. May be used for flashlight.
Conversion Filters	Amber	Kodak Type A Colour Negative, Eastmancolor Negative Type 5250, Ektachrome Commercial Type 7225 for daylight
85		
85B	Amber	Kodak Type B, daylight
85C	Amber	Kodak Type F and S, daylight
80B	Light blue	For exposing daylight-type colour materials in photoflood light. For panchromatic emulsions that reproduce red to light in tungsten light.

TABLE 13. *Orwo–Wolfen filters for colour negatives*

Filter	Colour	Use
K 14	Orange	For Orwocolor Negative Film NC 1 used in daylight.
K 18	Dark red–brown	
K 19	Orange	

3.12. COLOUR TEMPERATURE

There is an additional factor strongly affecting colour negatives and that is the colour temperature of the light source, which has a great influence on the accuracy of colour reproduction. In monochromes the colour temperature is not so important, because colours are reproduced in grey tones. The colour negative reproduces colours most faithfully in that region of colour temperature for which it has been balanced. The daylight film reproduces colours best when it is exposed to daylight, and the colour negative for artificial light produces the truest colours when exposed to artificial light. When a colour negative for daylight is used in artificial light a correction filter must be used over the camera lens, a blue one in this case, as otherwise the negative would reproduce green as yellow–green. If, on the other hand, negative for artificial lighting is exposed in daylight without a filter, green shows up as blue–green.

The colour temperature of a light source is expressed in degrees Kelvin. The higher the temperature, the bluer the light, the lower the temperature, the redder the light. This relation applies only to visual effects, but does not express how the temperature affects the colour negative. The majority of colour negatives reproduce the colours most faithfully at 3200°K. This temperature must therefore be maintained during filming as colour distortion would otherwise appear.

Many types of conversion filters have been developed for correcting the colour temperature, for the latter is a most important factor in colour reproduction. Tables 14–17 show some of them.

TABLE 14. *Conversion of colour temperature to 3200°K*

Colour temperature of source in K°	Filters required
2490	82C + 82C
2570	82C + 82B
2650	82C + 82A
2720	82C + 82
2800	82C
2900	82B
3000	82A
3100	82
3300	81
3400	81A
3500	81B
3600	81C
3850	81EF

TABLE 15. *Conversion of colour temperature to 3400°K*

Colour temperature of source in K°	Filters required
2610	82C + 82C
2700	82C + 82B
2780	82C + 82A
2870	82C + 82
2950	82C
3060	82B
3180	82A
3290	82
3510	81
3630	81A
3740	81B
3850	81C
4140	81EF

Filters of the 81 series are light brown and reduce high colour temperature of the light source; filters of the 82 series are blue and increase low colour temperature.

TABLE 16. *Kodak Wratten conversion filters (to be inserted in front of light source)*

Filters	Number	Use
I.L. Blue	548/2	Converts light from 3200°K lamps to approximate daylight
W.F. Green	555/3	Absorbs ultraviolet from high intensity carbon arcs and converts this light to approximate daylight
L.C.T. Yellow	558/11	Converts light of low colour temperature to 3200°K
W.F. Orange	558/13	Converts light of high colour temperature to 3200°K

TABLE 17. *Gevacolor CT Filters for Gevacolor Negative Type 652*

Illumination	Colour temperature	Filters
Studio photofloods	2800	—
Projection or over-run lamps	3200	—
Over-run lamps	3400	—
Daylight, 2 hours before sunrise or sunset	5000	CTO 8
Sun or blue sky	6000	CTO 12
Shade, 1–2 hr before or after sunset	6000	CTO 12
Clouds, overcast	7000	CTO 12
Shade, blue sky	10·000–12·000	CTO 12
Arclight	5500	CTO 12

The Gevaert Company produce two types of correction filters for adjusting the colour temperature. They are CTB filters for increasing colour temperature and CTO filters for reducing it.

4. MASK DESIGN

4.1. THE APPROACH

Film, theatre and television performances are always the result of the teamwork of artists and technical personnel. This union of artists and technicians is typical for the expression of dramatic art today and it demands great artistic discipline of all the people involved if a work of art impressive in its integrity, yet maintaining and expressing the ideas of the individual artists, is to be created.

The leading man in the team is the producer. All others must respect his dramatic conception of the play or scenario. Each member of the team studies the scenario from his individual point of view and by mutual discussion the rough outlines of a performance or a film gradually take shape.

The make-up artist must concentrate his attention upon a thorough analysis of the individual characters presented in the performance. He must make himself familiar with the environment and the period in which the characters live, with the dramatist's idea, and with the general concept of the performance.

The correct appreciation of the atmosphere of the literary pattern is most important for the faithful portrayal of the characters concerned. Each historical epoch and each type of community requires a specific means of expression and a specific approach.

In a historical play the fashion of that time must be known and respected, together with all the peculiarities typical of the particular country the characters are living in and for their social standing. It is vital to bear this in mind especially in historical dramas for the differences between the social classes were extremely marked in dress, hair style, etc. — far more than they are at present.

The make-up artist must always see that the faithful historical features in the appearance of the characters are in harmony with the personality of the actor or actress representing them. Sometimes he cannot venture to make up the actor exactly according to the fashion of the historical period in question. In the fifteenth century, for example, a very high forehead was considered beautiful. Women used to shave off a lot of hair in front, thus exposing the frontal bone almost completely. The eyebrows were plucked and high arches of new eyebrows were traced in thin lines on the forehead. The make-up man can seldom create a mask of this kind for any actress. He must always try to find a certain compromise between the historical truth and the possibilities at his disposal in order to give the spectators the illusion of an absolutely faithful historical mask, in keeping with the present-day ideals of beauty and sense of proportion.

The costumes, hair styles and the entire conception of masks for the individual characters of a historical play or film are designed by artists. Make-up artists usually design masks for contemporary films and plays, and take part in discussions dealing with the choice of the right type of actors for certain characters, for sometimes only a certain actor can be chosen for a certain part from the point of view of the make-up man. This very often happens when the play or film portrays the whole — or a greater part — of a person's life. Not every actor or actress can play such a part, because his or her type does not lend itself to make-up that successfully suggests gradual ageing.

4.2. CO-OPERATION OF THE MAKE-UP MAN WITH THE ACTOR

In the theatre and in television the cast is usually known beforehand, so that the designer and the make-up man design and create the mask for an already known actor. In film, however, a mask for the particular character is designed first and actors are chosen according to the results of rehearsals. The final appearance of the mask must then be completed in detail for the actor who has been selected as most suitable during rehearsals.

The daily contact of the make-up man with the actor is a valuable guide in creating the final shape of the mask, in which he has to consider all the characteristics of the actor's face at rest and in motion, so as to make the mask natural and convincing, especially with regard to close-up shots.

The producer, the actor and the make-up man analyse the character in question, his age, environment, social standing, hobbies, profession and any other factors that may affect his appearance and behaviour, because it is a knowledge of these details that helps the make-up man to create a faithful and convincing mask.

The film make-up man must also know which type of film negative will be used, coloured or monochromatic, wide-angled or of classical width, because each of these types requires a slightly different make-up technique; the lighting which differs according to the type and speed of the negatives considerably affects the colour tones of the make-up. He must act in close co-operation with the camera operator and the lighting man, as lighting can either dramatize make-up or mar its effects entirely.

The make-up man has to study all the modern methods of make-up, as well as all the technical novelties likely to have any bearing upon the results of his work, such as new ideas concerning lighting, the speed and properties of the more modern negatives and other items of a similar kind.

The producer as well as the camera operator makes the most of close-up shots, which help to dramatize certain situations. This, of course requires the greatest skill, meticulous care and precision on the part of the make-up man, because close-up shots show every detail of his work most clearly. It must, however, remain quite imperceptible and its results have to appear most natural particularly in the close-up shots, where none of his interventions can be detected. This is particularly difficult to achieve when plastic accessories of foamed latex must be used to alter the shape of the actor's face, or wigs and other hairpieces to change his hair.

It is quite obvious that the art of modern make-up requires great skill and artistic imagination as well as a deep knowledge of many technical aspects of film making.

4.3. THE DESIGN

Generally speaking, less usually means more in make-up. It is not always necessary to create a mask for every actor and every part. Sometimes, mainly in modern plays and films, the attention of the spectators is distracted from acting by unneccessary or exaggerated make-up.

Make-up is used for several purposes, of course, but the most important purpose is that it helps to adjust the colouring of the actor's complexion to the lighting and sensitivity of the negatives. There is no general rule for mask designing and making. Certain parts may be played by a number of actors of quite different types.

A good aid, however, for any mask design and for choosing the most suitable wigs, hairpieces or plastic accessories, is the following: a good photograph of the actor's face is divided with two lines into three equal vertical parts and with four lines into three equal horizontal parts.

The first horizontal line runs along the hairline, the second between the brow bone and the edge of the upper lid, the third line runs below the tip of the nose and the fourth touches the chin. The vertical lines are at right-angles to the horizontal ones and are in the centre of the eyes and cheeks. This division of the face into nine areas enables the make-up artist to perceive instantly any irregularities in the actor's face. If the nose is too long, or the chin too big, or the forehead too high, it appears clearly in the individual fields. Narrow or broad eyes are also very obvious, so that the make-up man sees clearly which parts need corrective make-up and which can be made up in a normal way (Fig. 14).

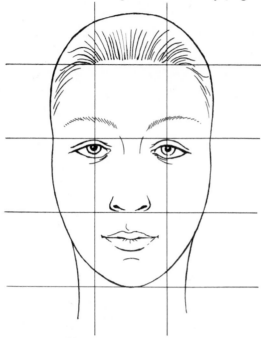

FIG. 14. The division of the face with horizontal and vertical lines into nine approximately uniform areas.

If the required mask is a more complicated one, it is best to use the actor's unretouched portrait photographs, *en face* and both profiles. If the shape of the head or of the ears or neck is to be altered, another photograph, showing the back of the actor's head, must be used. The profile photographs are very important, because sometimes even a slight change of the profile may result in a surprising change of the entire appearance of the face (Figs. 15–18).

The required mask is outlined in the photograph. It is advisable to do that when a mask of an authentic character is designed, because such a mask usually requires the use of foamed latex parts. With the help of the drawing on the photograph the parts of the face that need the latex accessories are clearly seen. A more detailed design of the mask is then drawn, the photograph serving as a pattern. A wig and hairpieces are made according to the design, and, if necessary, foamed latex accessories are prepared. Last and most important is the stage of make-up and creating the mask on the actor's face.

45

FIGS. 15–18. THE DESIGN OF A MASK

Fig. 15. The artistic design.

Fig. 16. The actor's photograph.

Fig. 17. The required changes outlined in the photograph.

Fig. 18. The resulting mask.

5. THE PRINCIPLES OF MAKE-UP

MAKE-UP is an essential and inevitable part of the actor's expression and must never be underestimated.

Perfect make-up is a very complicated matter demanding detailed study, long training and practice. It is quite a serious problem, for a performance can either gain very much by good make-up or lose much if the make-up is bad. Wrong make-up ruins a part much more than an unsuitable costume.

In the film and television studios and in big theatres the actors are made up in special rooms or in their dressing rooms. Extreme cleanliness of these rooms must always be stressed very strongly because the actor's complexion is greatly strained by make-up and is apt to get infected. Regular hygienic supervision of all the aids and implements for make-up should be a matter of routine.

Film and television studios have a good standard in this respect, but the situation is, however, much worse in smaller theatres of amateur theatrical groups.

5.1. MAKE-UP AND COMPLEXION

The principles of modern cosmetics are simple and accessible to anybody. First of all, it is cleanliness of the body, proper nourishment and suitable care and treatment of the skin.

The actor, whose complexion is exposed to almost constant strain and irritation, should pay close attention to it and care for it accordingly. He should at least know the type of his skin, so that he can restore it to normal after removing the make-up and thus reduce to a minimum the unfavourable effects of his profession on his complexion.

Normal healthy skin is fresh and elastic and the strain caused by make-up seldom harms it. A different situation arises, however, in case of dry or oily skin or sensitive skin, which sometimes react quite unexpectedly to various external factors.

The complexion can vary in different parts of the face. It is, however, quite impossible to consider and treat the different types of complexion during making-up in the theatre, film and television studios. The main aim of professional make-up is to achieve maximum likeness with the type and character the actor is to represent. Even if modern cosmetics are prepared according to proper standards, their main aim is to achieve the best aesthetic effect. A greasy foundation is usually employed in most cases regardless of the respective types of complexion.

Many external factors in the studio or on the stage have unfavourable and irritating effects on the skin, and the make-up man should know something about them.

Light emitted by the arc lights is very rich in infrared radiations which are warm and irritating to the skin. In addition to that, there are a number of other factors harmful to the skin, such as dust, frequent interventions of the make-up man repairing the make-up, constant nervous strain, etc. All these factors show that the skin deserves thorough care and treatment.

The epidermis is a very complicated and sensitive system which has to be carefully treated, according to its skin type.

The following principles can, and should, be respected by anybody who wants to keep the skin healthy.

There are four basic types of complexion—normal, dry, oily and sensitive.

Normal complexion is dry around the eyes and on the cheeks, whereas the forehead, nose and chin are a little oily.

Oily skin is shiny, the pores are open and it looks coarsely textured. Pimples and blackheads appear in some areas after irritation.

Dry complexion is lacking in water and fatty content. It wrinkles soon, especially around the eyes and mouth. Sometimes the skin peels in tiny flakes.

Sensitive complexion reacts readily to many external effects, the skin reddens and colour spots appear.

It is necessary to cleanse the complexion thoroughly twice a day, in the morning and in the evening. Air pollution, especially in big cities is so dense that a thin film of soot and dust settles on the face and may irritate the skin. The respiration of the pores is blocked and various skin infections may appear. The skin should be cleaned with a cleansing cream or lotion, twice as a rule, to clean the blocked pores thoroughly. Cleansing lotion or cream dissolves the dirt in the pores. The cleansers should be lightly patted on the skin either with the finger-tips or with a moist pad of cotton wool, and the surplus removed with tissues. Cleansing should be started under the chin and carried on upward to the cheeks and forehead. After cleansing it is advisable to rinse the face with luke-warm water.

A tonic suitable for the particular type of skin should then be applied to the skin to remove a thin film of the cleansing cream, to contract the open pores, to increase blood circulation, and to give the skin a fresh look.

A moisturizing cream or lotion should then be applied to supply the skin with the necessary amount of moisture and to provide a protecting film on the complexion. It is also an excellent base for the make-up. Make-up should never be applied on dry skin without previous application of a moisturizing cream.

Careful preparation of the skin before the application of make-up is very important. The face should be quite clean, completely free from previous make-up and grease. Men should be clean shaven. Some shaving soaps, especially alkaline ones, soften the beard but irritate and dehydrate the skin too much. It is better to use shaving creams or an electric shaver.

Make-up should be removed very carefully, slowly and gently. It is best to use cleansing lotions of good quality. *Vaseline* is not suitable as it is very oily. Healthy complexion is extremely important for the actor and he should try to avoid all unnecessary strain such as stretching the skin around the eyes and mouth and thus helping to form wrinkles and lines. The face should never be dried with a rough towel. The best way is to press a soft facecloth lightly to the face and blot off the water.

After complete removal of all make-up the complexion should be treated according to its type. Massages, Turkish baths, exercise in the open air, sunbathing, sound sleep and proper nourishment are the basic factors of good health and fresh looks.

5.2. IS MAKE-UP NECESSARY?

Sometimes people ask if make-up is really necessary in film, television, and on the stage. The answer is definitely an affirmative one, if the actor is to look natural in strong lighting, or if he is to represent a certain character in his performance.

Normal facial pigments appear uneven in the intense light illuminating the scene. All kinds of coloured spots, reddish noses and cheeks, bluish beard, red or brown freckles, spots and especially scars are much too apparent on the screen. Make-up conceals all these blemishes and of course, not only that. Skilfully applied make-up may even make a prominent nose, chin or jaw look smaller and gentler, eyes that are too narrow look wider. Make-up generally corrects many irregularities in the face.

Surprising changes may be achieved by suitable make-up, dress and lighting. However, it is always necessary to know the limits of the make-up artist's possibilities. There are certain effects that are impossible to achieve however hard the make-up man tries. For example, he cannot change a fat man into a thin one; a fat man may look slimmer, but not quite slim, just as a broad nose may look narrower, but never quite narrow. Some people, for example members of amateur groups, expect that the make-up artist will completely change the type of an actor into quite a different one that is just very much needed. This is, of course, quite impossible, just as it is impossible on the professional stage, as in film and television studios.

A face without make-up usually looks too "ordinary" because of minor cosmetic blemishes and defects. In some films, for example in crime stories, the effect of harsh reality may complete and emphasize the atmosphere but is undesirable in the majority of other films, because it mars the artistic effects of the actor's performance and diverts the attention of the audience.

Make-up helps to achieve a natural or better look, changes age, helps to interpret the dramatist's conception of a certain character, and corrects the effects of lighting and distance between the actor and his audience or a camera.

5.2.1. *Make-up on the Stage, in the Film and Television Studios*

There is a certain difference between the work of the make-up artist in the film and television studios and on the stage; this difference appears already in designing and creating a mask. These three media have many basic factors in common as far as the technique is concerned, but each of them has its own specific features that distinguish it from the other two.

The theatre performance takes 2, or at the most 3 hours, and it is usually impossible to make complicated changes of the actor's make-up within this time. A similar situation prevails in the television studio. This fact must be kept in mind while designing the mask, so that it is not too complicated and time-consuming, for sometimes the actor plays different parts in the afternoon and evening performances. The interval between the two performances (let alone the breaks within one performance!) is not very long and even in big theatres the actors make themselves up almost without any help of the make-up people; the time is too short to create a complicated mask using, for example, plastic accessories.

In no case must the actor or the make-up man rely upon the distance between the stage and audience to conceal a careless or exaggerated make-up. Stage make-up must always look perfectly natural to the audience. It must bridge the distance, and survive strong illumination which often bleaches the natural colours of the actor's face and which flattens some parts of it. Make-up must appear natural to the spectators in the first row as well as to those in the back rows. It is quite wrong to think that stage make-up needs thicker layers of make-up than for film. Good results are achieved by the right choice of suitable colour tones, well-balanced shadows and highlights, which must be carefully blended, especially the shadows on the eyelids and rouge on the cheeks. Wrinkles, furrows, hollows and other features may have deeper colours but must never be drawn in hard lines and should always be applied by the same technique as in film.

There is another factor, very important from the psychological point, that must be carefully considered. The actor's partner is his first critic, a very sensitive one, to any defect in his colleague's make-up. Subconsciously he must make quite a hard psychological effort to master the situation, and this strain more or less mars his own performance.

The work of the television make-up man is rather extraordinary compared with that in the film studio or theatre. The actor should be made-up as for close-up shots and at the same time as for the stage, i.e. his make-up should be more exaggerated. He is taken by three or more cameras which alternately take close-ups and panshots and thus replace the film cut. The performance is watched by the spectator on a small screen which would demand a heavier make-up, similar to that on the stage. This may be used, however, only in the so-called television theatres, i.e. theatres adapted for television use, which have flat, even lighting and where the cameras do not get too close to the actors.

Most of the television studios are illuminated by modelling light in addition to the main lighting and therefore the make-up should be fainter, more natural, i.e. similar to that in the film studio. The colour of the background which is often changed within one show is another important factor. Light background darkens the colours of the make-up, dark background lightens them.

The pick-up tubes used at present reproduce the colours into the tones of grey as faithfully as panchromatic film, so that nowadays the television make-up artist need not correct the unsuitable colour reproduction of the first camera pick-up tubes.

Ceiling-mounted lights make shadows under the eyebrows and eyes. To a limited extent this may be corrected by the use of a lighter foundation make-up applied on the shaded parts. Too light a tone, however, has much more unfavourable effects than the shadows. Generally the colour tones of all kinds of foundation make-up look almost similar in television.

Dry types of make-up are preferred in television, i.e. pancakes and pressed powders, because they stay longer on the face without any change. The actor must be made up before the dress rehearsal in the final illumination, so that the make-up can be checked before the camera, and the actor waits for the broadcast for several hours. Fatty make-up gets shiny and the colours are patchy. Very often the programmes follow each other so quickly in television that many actors have to apply the foundation themselves, because there are not enough make-up people to make up each actor individually. Pancake and pressed powder may be applied more quickly, colour blending is easier, so that with a minimum of skill it is possible to achieve relatively better results than with the fatty foundation. The make-up man then has more time left for those who have more complicated make-up and need his help.

Pink and orange lipsticks must be avoided in television make-up for these colours show up as very light grey tones and do not contrast with the surrounding complexion. A beard stick is a very frequently used indispensable implement for concealing the beard area when it is too pronounced. It is usually complexion-coloured; it should never be applied too generously as the face would look unnaturally smooth. All the other aids are the same as in film and theatre practice.

The working conditions of the film make-up artist differ from those of his colleagues in the television studio and in the theatre.

Let us look back to the beginnings of film, when the problem of using or omitting make-up was being discussed. The answer to this question is not settled and make-up has its definite and important position in filming. The reason why it is so is clearly seen in comparing a documentary with a feature film. There is a striking difference between the made up faces of actors in the feature film and the faces without any make-up in the documentary film. Natural pigment and tiny blood vessels are unevenly arrayed all over the face, causing a change of colour in some areas. Photographed without make-up the face records mottled and unnaturally dark in some places, especially in close-ups when the camera gets very near to the face of the actor. All skin blemishes and discolorations are then very obvious on the enlarged image on the screen. The strong illumination used in the studio and even out-of-doors also emphasizes all skin irregularities.

The main and the most important purpose of film make-up is to level the difference in the sensitivity to colours between the human eye and the film negative. Make-up must smooth the complexion and give the actor an even, healthy skin tone and dramatize his features, if necessary.

As a rule, the film actor never makes himself up as he would never be able to accomplish the complicated demands of film make-up. A make-up artist has to fulfil this difficult task which, in the film, is quite different from theatre practice. The work of the film make-up man is affected not only by the illumination, but also by the type and quality of the film negatives and, last but not least, by the manner of the camera-man.

If the theatre actor playing the same part for many successive evenings is not always made up exactly in the same way in every detail of his mask, not much harm can be done. It is necessary to maintain the character of the make-up but minor inaccuracies do not matter.

This, of course, will never do in the film. Films are made according to a scenario which is divided into certain scenes and individual shots, which are never filmed in successive order. Because filming takes many weeks and sometimes even months, it is absolutely necessary to maintain the original make-up of the actor for the whole period of filming. The make-up must be applied daily and must be exactly the same throughout filming, so that when the film is edited the individual shots fit together even as far as make-up is concerned.

The film make-up artist can correct the actor's make-up during filming. This is a precious advantage compared with the possibilities of his theatre and television colleagues, but the working hours are considerably longer as filming goes on for 8 to 10 hours a day and the make-up man must start to apply make-up at least one hour before the filming.

5.3. THE PRINCIPLES OF MAKE-UP

The same make-up applied to two different people need not always yield the same results. This is due to different types of skin texture with different pigmentation. The influence of varied amount of pigment on the resulting coloration of make-up may be illustrated by the following example. When we paint a brown slab and a red one with white paint the result will not be the same, because the different colour of the primer will affect the colour of the finishing coat. The colour of the human complexion differs in the amount of pigment, tiny blood vessels and the transparency of the skin.

Foundation make-up is exactly the same in film, television and on the stage. Only the colours and technique of application change according to the film material (monochromatic or coloured) and the environment. The basic colour tones of foundation make-up should always correspond with the colours of the actor's face. Make-up should always be applied in a thin layer.

If dark or olive-coloured complexion is to be made paler the face is toned according to the lightest areas, mostly to the areas around the eyes. Suitable make-up a shade lighter than the skin is carefully applied, especially for a colour film. A colour film ruthlessly betrays the original colour of the complexion and if the colours of the make-up do not match it, photography reveals all the make-up artist's interference in the face of the actor.

5.4. FOUNDATION MAKE-UP

Foundation make-up is used to provide the colours of the entire face, the throat, the ears and the shoulders. Any type of make-up such as fatty foundation, emulsion make-up and liquid powder or pancake may be used as foundation make-up.

Foundation make-up is applied to the face, throat and ears in a very thin layer with the fingertips or with a fine, slightly moistened rubber sponge. It is best to start on the forehead, as its broad surface easily shows the right thickness of the make-up layer.

Make-up must be applied absolutely evenly, without any blobs, or leaving patches of naked skin without any make-up. Special care must be taken in making up the parts that are in the shade, i.e. under the chin and on the throat. After foundation make-up has been applied, the face should be lightly patted with the finger-tips dipped in luke-warm water. This technique blends any colour spots or other irregularities, make-up is absorbed better by the skin and it is more resistant to mechanical damage. The throat, shoulders and hands are not made up with the fatty foundation, because the costumes might be soiled and liquid powder, transparent make-up or pancake are used instead. They are applied with a moistened sponge.

5.5. SHADOWING AND CONTOURING

After the foundation make-up has been applied, the prominent parts of the face, or those that appear flat or depressed, are retouched or contoured with darker toned make-up to conceal the former, and with light make-up to emphasize the latter parts of the face, so that the final appearance should be well balanced. Men usually have square jaws and more prominent features than women. Broad jaws and high cheek bones may appear narrower and less obvious if darker shadows are applied to them; double chins may be made less apparent, a broad nose may appear narrower, etc. Auxiliary make-up three or four shades darker than the foundation may be used but it must correspond with it in the basic colour tone. To shadow large areas, such as high cheek bones, broad jaws, high foreheads or double chins, make-up is applied by light patting with the finger-tips. The shadows must be carefully blended with the foundation, and must be made very faint. Highlights are applied on the flat and depressed areas with light toned auxiliary make-up by the same technique. The light tones must also harmonize with the foundation make-up.

Pronounced dark rings under the eyes, which are signs of fatigue, illness or age, wrinkles and various skin blemishes are usually covered with light-toned make-up or with a covering cream before the application of foundation make-up. This is safer, because discolorations of the complexions may appear in the strong light of film and television studios even under the foundation make-up. When the covering cream is used, its colour must correspond with the colour of the complexion and not with the colour of the foundation make-up.

The make-up man judges the progress of his work on the actor's image in the mirror and slowly rotates the actor's head to see where deepest shades appear. With a fine brush he applies light make-up on the spots in the darkest shadow to avoid strong contrasts.

Contouring for colour film must be done with the utmost care, because careless shadowing of a broad jaw, for example, may appear as an incompletely shaven chin.

5.6. FIXING WITH POWDER

After the application of foundation make-up, lips must be carefully cleaned to remove all traces of make-up and the foundation is fixed by powdering. The parts around the eyes are patted first with the finger-tips to smooth the faint wrinkles which sometimes appear in the make-up and which are caused by the movements of the eyelids.

Powder is applied first around the eyes, and then to the rest of the face, the throat and the ears. This process completes perfect blending of all colours of the foundation and auxiliary make-up, and all shiny areas that may sometimes appear in the face are also concealed. The powder fixes make-up to the skin so that it is more resistant to damage and is not easily smeared. The powder should always be a shade lighter than the foundation, because powder pigments darken when they come in contact with fatty make-up.

Light foundation make-up cannot be made darker by using dark powder, because it causes dark blotches which spoil the appearance and are very obvious on the screen.

FIG. 19. The application of powder with a powder-puff.

55

Powder should be always applied with fairly large powder-puffs by light patting and never by rubbing, as the foundation make-up might get smeared (Fig. 19). Surplus powder can be removed with a powder brush (Fig. 20). If it is necessary to achieve a slight shine in the face, it is advisable to moisten the skin with a fine sponge or with moist finger-tips.

FIG. 20. Brushing off surplus of powder.

For old-age make-up it is best to use talcum powder which is sufficiently transparent so that shadows and highlights on the face are not completely covered. The face achieves a translucent whitish tint.

Before the final make-up is completed, all traces of foundation make-up and powder must be removed from the hair, the eyebrows and lashes with a good, sharp brush.

5.7. MAKE-UP OF CHILDREN

A child loses its typical natural appearance when too striking a make-up is used. Children should not, therefore, be made up at all, but it is necessary to adjust the colour of the complexion to suit the lighting which each particular studio or production may use, and to level the appearance of all the performers in this respect. In no case, however, must the make-up distort the frank, innocent expression of the child's face. Very subtle foundation is therefore used, lips are cleaned well and the eyebrows are carefully brushed to enhance their natural line. If really necessary, eyebrow make-up is applied very sparingly indeed. The eyes of children are relatively big and very expressive. Any eye make-up used to enhance the eyes adds age to the child's face.

Freckles are very often a characteristic feature of children's faces and should be concealed only when absolutely necessary.

A slight amount of pastel toned rouge may be applied on the cheeks for colour film and for the stage. The rouge is applied on the cheeks and not on the cheek bones, as is usual in the adult face.

Lipstick, if any, should always be applied very sparingly.

5.8. ERRORS IN THE APPLICATION OF MAKE-UP

The same errors are very often repeated, namely if the actor has to apply make-up himself without any help of the make-up man, or in unfavourable conditions, or when he has very little time for a quick make-up change.

Most frequently the area near the hairline on the forehead and on the temples lacks make-up, the arms, the throat, or the neck are carelessly made up; layers are too heavy or shadows are too obvious, highlights and rouge are also applied.

Very often all the natural lustre of the skin is concealed and the final result is matt. The natural lustre should be maintained as a matt finish photographs very flat. A shine can be achieved by patting dried make-up with a moist sponge, or by blotting grease-paint with a dry sponge. Powder should be very sparingly used in the make-up of men.

5.9. HOW TO REMOVE MAKE-UP

The make-up man should never remove make-up off the actor's face. He should remove only wigs and the other hairpieces and plastic accessories after previously moistening the edges with alcohol, and the residues of adhesives. He should, however, never remove other make-up. The actor should do it himself, very carefully and gently. This is very important for the skin, which has been strained for many hours, when the layers of make-up, adhesives, the hairpieces or a wig, and possibly foamed rubber accessories blocked the pores and limited the respiration of the skin.

Make-up removers should be chosen according to the type of make-up used. Water-soluble make-up such as translucent and emulsion make-up or liquid powder are easily removed by washing with water and mild soap. Grease-paint and other fatty make-up must be removed with a make-up removing lotion. The unpleasant feeling of oily skin, which is left on the face after fatty make-up, may be removed with a lotion containing a higher amount of alcohol. Adhesive residues are removed with diluted alcohol.

The actor's care for his skin should not finish by removing make-up. Complete skin care depends on the type of the skin and should be performed after consulting a dermatologist.

5.10. AMATEUR THEATRICAL GROUPS

The conditions of the amateur theatrical groups are different from those of the professional theatre. The amateurs almost always make themselves up without any help from an experienced make-up man or from a professional actor. They must rely on their own taste, imagination, estimation of possibilities and skill. Amateurs should always consider very carefully the situation of the play they are going to perform and they should thoroughly study all the inner and outer signs of the characters, so as to avoid errors, very frequent and typical for amateur theatrical groups. It is the tendency of many amateurs to represent an entirely different character, corresponding to their own idea of beauty, regardless of the true characteristics of the performed part, and very often regardless of their own physical type. This leads them to exaggerate make-up, which then looks unnatural. Amateur actresses usually try to look very young, taking no notice whatsoever of their own disposition. The resulting character is distorted and unconvincing. These mistakes are enhanced by the very short distance between the stage and the audience in small theatres.

Every amateur should consider all these facts carefully and in case his part does not require a complicated mask he should emphasize his natural expression and with the help of sensibly used make-up he should enhance certain features of his face, so as to express most faithfully the character he has to represent. He must realize that he does not have the capabilities of the professional actor or of the make-up artist, whose skill is the result of many years' experience and studies.

6. THE TECHNIQUE OF MAKE-UP

THE eyes, the nose, the mouth and the lips are the most important features in the face and therefore attract most of the spectator's attention. After completing the foundation make-up of the face, the make-up man tries to emphasize the respective parts with suitable make-up maintaining, however, the most desirable harmony of the entire face. The complete make-up must be well balanced and must faithfully portray the character represented.

The individual facial parts are made-up in a very similar way for film and television as well as for the stage. Minor changes which are sometimes observed in the technique are due to different working conditions, as has been mentioned elsewhere in this book. The make-up man must always respect the dominant demand for achieving the most natural appearance of the actors and he must adjust the make-up to the character of lighting used either on the stage or in the studio, where—in addition to lighting—he must also regard the quality, sensitivity and other characteristics of the film negatives.

6.1. THE EYES

The eyes express most faithfully all human emotions and feelings, and therefore greatly affect the expression of the face. Correct make-up of the eyes is the most difficult part of make-up, because any interference is very obvious. The make-up man must be exceedingly careful and devote most of his attention to proper make-up of the eyes from the beginning of applying the foundation make-up.

The eyes are two identical objects situated in the face close to each other, the shape of one being the mirror image of the other and they must therefore be made-up in exactly the same way. This is most important especially for close-up shots in film and television.

It is advisable to make-up the left eye first and then the right eye. If the right eye is made up first, the hand blocks the view while making-up the left one and thus comparing the results of make-up on both eyes is more difficult. (This rule, of course, applies only to right-handed people, left-handed ones should start with applying make-up on the right eye.) A proper application of the foundation make-up is the most important phase of the work in the make-up of the lower lid. Usually a fatty foundation, a shade lighter than the one for the entire face, is used, and it is applied right to the edge of the eye socket by gentle patting. Care must be taken not to stretch the fine skin of the lid too much, as tiny lines would appear. If the type of make-up requires smearing, stroking should be very gentle. Pressed powder, which is sometimes used as a foundation for young country girls, is applied with a soft brush (Fig. 21).

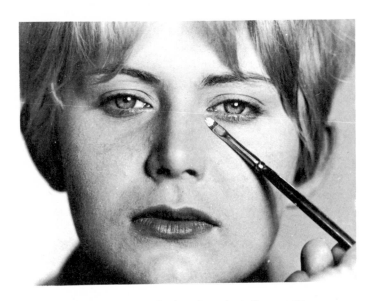

FIG. 21.   The application of powder to the eye area.

Sometimes, however, it is necessary to change the size, shape and expression of the eyes in order to achieve a better portrait of a certain character. The type of the role, and the art of the particular actor, are the best guides for the make-up man in creating a mask. He must never forget, however, that each part and each actor have to be treated individually because a certain way of make-up, excellent in one part, would be ridiculous in another. For example, a country girl cannot have her eyes shadowed and false lashes applied in the same way as an aristocratic woman or a model.

Women, however, must have their eyes made up in all cases. Narrow eyes or thin and short eyelashes must be lined, because some types of eyes are expressionless without suitably applied shadows, lines and even false eyelashes. Faint shadows around the eyes contrast well with make-up and the white of the eye. In the make-up for young, plain girls, eyes should be emphasized only very subtly.

6.1.1. *The Eye-line*

Sharp eyebrow pencils or small brushes (pointed or flat) are used as eye-liners. The upper, as well as the lower, eyelids should always be lined with dark brown or dark grey pencils. The black ones are used chiefly on the stage. Black eye-lines are used very rarely in film and television, only in cases where exceptionally expressive eyes are required. However, only the upper eyelids are lined with a black eye-liner (Figs. 22 and 23).

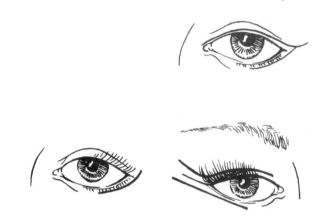

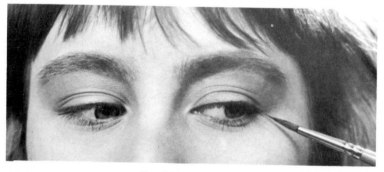

FIG. 22.   The eye-line.

FGI. 23.   The eye-line.

In earlier years when orthochromatic emulsions were used, the colour of the foundation make-up appeared almost as white as the white of the eye. The eyes were quite expressionless without marked shadowing. Blue or red–brown shadows were applied on the upper eyelid from the bridge of the nose to the eyebrows. This fashion was also largely used on the stage and, as a matter of fact, it has been maintained in some theatres to the present day, because some actors think that eyes made-up in this way are more expressive; that, of course, is completely fallacious.

The lower eyelid should be lined with a brown pencil; black would provide an unnatural effect, because the eyelashes on the lower lid are shorter and thinner than those on the upper eyelid. Recently, because of the influence of television, blue or grey–blue shadows are used for the upper eyelids, as the contours are softer.

The most suitable colour for eye make-up is chosen after photographic tests have been carried out in the studio or after judging the colours visually in the required lighting on the stage. At first, the eyelids of the left eye are lined close to the eyelashes. The lines enlarge the eye and emphasize its expression; the colour of the lines should either correspond to the colour of the eyebrows and lashes or to the colour of the eyes. The final effect is different in each case. The line should be drawn as close to the lashes as possible and should be extended at the outer corner a little upwards to the temple. The line on the lower eyelid does not start right in the inner corner but a little towards the centre of the lid. It is also drawn to the outer corner of the eye and should never converge with the upper line (Fig. 22).

6.1.2. Eye-shadows

Correct colour of eye-shadows must be chosen according to the type. Eye-shadows change the expression of the eyes, enhance the colour of the iris, and give the eyes either a fresh or tired, old-looking appearance. The colour of the iris must always be the darkest in the make-up, otherwise the eyes look weary. Dark eye-shadows should never be used for pale eyes. as the colour of the make-up would suppress the colour of the eye and the final result would appear unnatural. Eye-shadows are usually made in pastel colours, such as grey–blue, grey–green, brown, or in colours that have a slight golden or silver lustre. These types enhance the original colour of the eye very well.

An impression of very heavy eyelids is achieved by application of very light grey–green or silver eye-shadows on the edge of the eyelids, and by very dark shadows applied on the ridge between the brows and the lid. Sometimes more colours are combined. Blue eye-shadow can blend with brown towards the brow, or brown shadow applied close to the lashes can fade into beige when blended towards the brow. The eyes seem deeper. The eye-line may be blue, brown or even black. To enlarge the eyes, very light shadows should be applied and blended towards the brow. It is advisable to use green eye-shadow and brown eye-line for pale eyes. The green shadow is blended into the complexion colour towards the brows.

For shows, music-hall performances, or in film shots of such scenes, eye-shadows with golden shines may be applied close to the eyelashes to achieve the impression of sparkling eyes.

Recently women emphasized their eyes in a similar manner to that used for eye make-up by ballet dancers. The eye-lines are extended

FIGS. 24 AND 25. EYELASH MAKE-UP

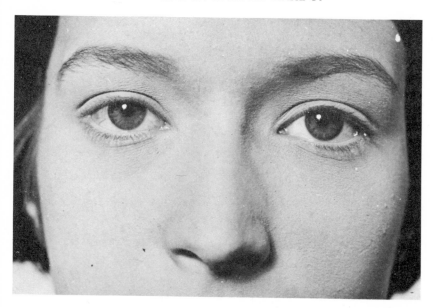

FIG. 24. The eye without make-up.

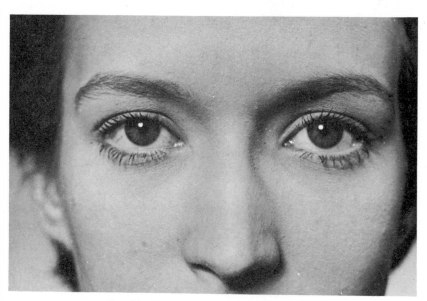

FIG. 25. The eyelashes enhanced with mascara.

FIGS. 26 AND 27. EYELASH MAKE-UP

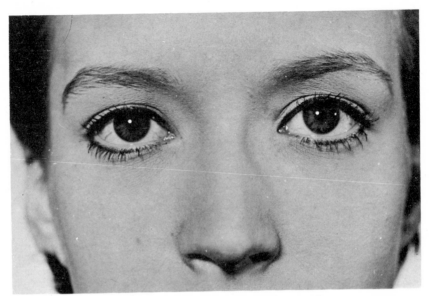

FIG. 26. Made up eyelashes with enhanced eye-line.

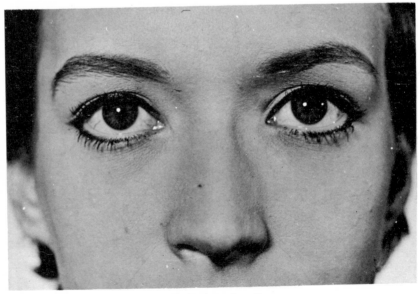

FIG. 27. Prolonged eye-line.

beyond the eye itself in the outer corner and directed upwards to the temple. This type of eye-line is sometimes also used for portraying certain characters in film and television. Eye-shadows are produced in a variety of colours in the form of fatty auxiliary make-up or pastes. The pastes are usually applied together with the foundation make-up. They are either applied only the eyelids or are blended upwards on the brows.

6.1.3. *Mascara*

Mascara is applied very sparingly on the lashes to avoid making the lashes sticky. When generously applied, small particles of make-up fall off the lashes and soil the surrounding of the eye. Sometimes, if the mascara is not completely dry it may smear on the lids and thus form unwanted shadows. These shadows should be carefully removed with a wad of moist cotton-wool. If the make-up gets in the eye it stings and irritates the conjunctiva.

Eyelash make-up is applied on closed eyes. The upper lid is stretched a little with the fingers so as to bring the lashes apart and the make-up is applied with a brush or a plastic spiral, at the same time curling the lashes upwards as required. On the lower lashes make-up is applied very sparingly indeed; because dark shadows would appear under the eyes and the final effect would be too unnatural. If the lower lashes are thick and dark it is not necessary to use make-up at all as the eye-line enhances the eye sufficiently. On the upper lashes, however, make-up must be almost always applied; sometimes it is even advisable to line the upper lid more markedly. Eyelash make-up is always applied to the lashes before false lashes are fixed in place. Some eyelashes do not curl upwards and it is therefore necessary to curl them with the help of the eyelash curler. This is always done before any make-up is applied. Care must be taken not to pinch the skin of the eyelid (Figs. 24–27).

Recently plastic spirals have been used to apply mascara for liquid types of eyelash make-up. These aids curl the lashes at the same time and application is much easier and safer, because make-up cannot get into the eye, and neither can it soil the surroundings of the eyes.

Liquid eyelash make-up containing fine filaments is applied only with spiral brushes. The fibres stick to the ends of the lashes and lengthen them sufficiently so that there is no need for false lashes to be used. This is most welcome to any make-up man, because fixing false lashes is a much more complicated matter.

The plastic spiral is held vertically when make-up is applied to the upper lashes and horizontally to make-up the shorter, lower lashes. The spiral brushes for the application of the lash lengthener, containing fine filaments, are held transversally to the lashes.

There are two types of eyelash make-up—one is soluble in water and the other is resistant to water; both are either liquid or solid. The water-resistant type should always be used for film and television as it does not smear and soil the foundation make-up.

6.1.4. *False Eyelashes*

False eyelashes may be used if the actress has too thin or too short lashes of her own. False lashes should always have the same shape as the natural ones. Not only do they enhance the beauty of the eye but they can also change its expression entirely and are therefore an important aid for corrective make-up.

False lashes are cut with a small pair of scissors to fit the width of the eye, or, if they are too long, they are trimmed to the required length and shape. Adhesive is applied to the strip holding the lashes. The lashes are then laid on the natural lashes and fit exactly in the inner corner. The strip holding the lashes must touch the base of the natural lashes and no skin must appear between the strip and the base. The strip is then gently pressed to the edge of the eyelid towards the outer corner where it should follow the line of the natural lashes; to enhance the eye-line more markedly, the false lashes may turn slightly upwards to the temple. The strip holding the false lashes is made up by drawing a line along it with a sharp brush (Fig. 28).

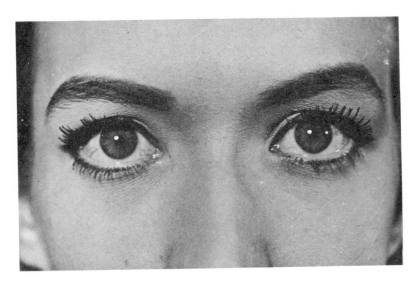

FIG. 28. False eyelashes.

After the false lashes have been fixed the eye-line is drawn and is slightly lengthened from the outer corner upwards.

6.1.5. *The Eyebrows*

The eyebrows, as marked features of the eye area, also affect the character and appearance of the face. By suitable shaping of the brows the eyes may acquire either a happy or a grim expression (Fig. 29).

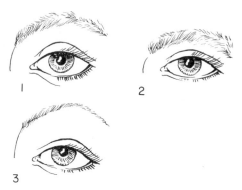

FIG. 29. The eyebrows. 1. The natural line of the eyebrows harmonizing with the shape of the eye. 2. Broader and lowered eyebrows make the eye appear broader. 3. Narrow and arched eyebrows make the eye appear narrower.

When brows are shaped and made up, the colour of the hair, the shape of the eyes, and the width and height of the forehead must be taken into account. The colour of the brows should always correspond to the colour of the hair and complexion, and to the colour of eye-shadows. Black-haired or platinum blonde women may have completely black eyebrows; in some cases also the red-haired women, supposing the colour of the eyes is matching. It is not necessary to enhance the colour of the brows too much when the hair is brown or blonde. In these cases the eyebrows are shaped according to the shape of the eyes and type of the face.

The roundness of a round face is enhanced by thick, markedly arched brows. A broad face may appear narrower, if not too thick brows are arched upwards in the outer third of their length. A long face may seem shorter when the brows are thick, well marked, but not too arched. The shape and thickness of the brows must also correspond to the shape of the lips. Thin lips, for example, do not harmonize with thick, broad eyebrows and arched eyebrows do not match with thin, straight lips. Thick and regular brows do not usually need any make-up; it is sufficient to brush them into the required shape and apply a little face cream. The arch of the brows should correspond to the shape of the eyes. A high forehead and high cheek bones require brows arched from the bridge of the nose. The eyebrows should be brushed into their natural shape before any shape changes take place.

If the ends of the brows are upturned the expression of the eye is a

FIGS. 30–36. MAKE-UP OF THE EYEBROWS

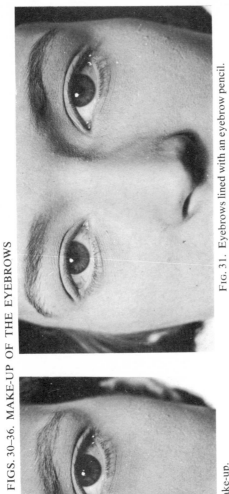

FIG. 30. Eyebrows without make-up.

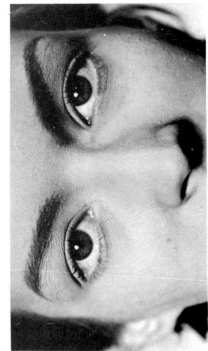

FIG. 31. Eyebrows lined with an eyebrow pencil.

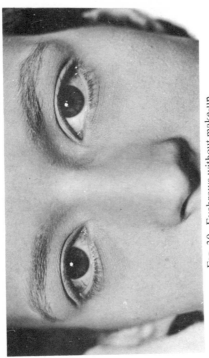

FIG. 32. Eyebrows with generously applied make-up.

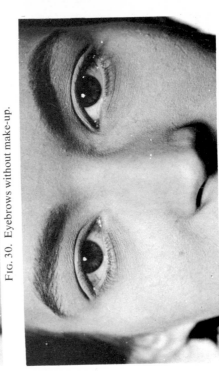

FIG. 33. Narrowed and arched eyebrows.

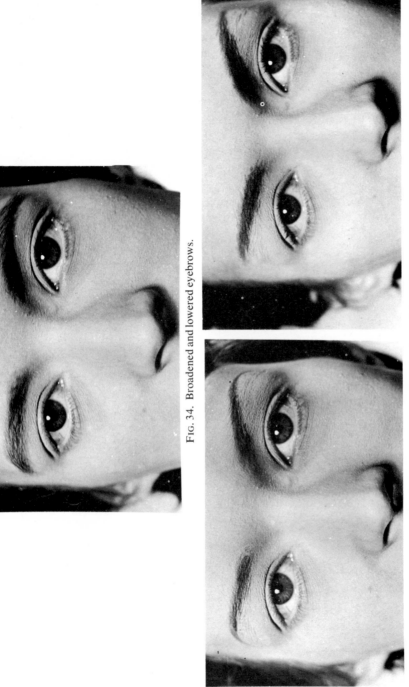

FIG. 34. Broadened and lowered eyebrows.

FIGS. 35 and 36. Altered shape of the eyebrows.

69

smiling one; if the ends are turned down at the outer corner of the eye, it looks grim.

The make-up alterations should never be exaggerated and should always correspond to the original appearance of the brows. Low set or too broad eyebrows are plucked on the lower edge. The brows should form an unbroken line and all surplus hair, that sometimes make them look a little shaggy at the outer ends, should be removed. The brows should not be plucked at the bridge of the nose.

The eyebrows are drawn with a sharp eyebrow pencil to conceal thin spots. It is also possible to use eyelash make-up applied with a spiral brush. The brows appear much thicker and have the same colour as the lashes (Figs. 30–36).

Make-up is applied to the lashes and brows after the face has been completely made up and powdered.

6.1.6. *Corrective Eye Make-up*

Eyes that are to express fatigue, age or illness must be made-up very carefully. The elasticity of the complexion in the vicinity of the eye depends upon the amount of fat and water in the subcutaneous tissue. In the lower lid this tissue usually loses water during illness, the capillaries of the skin are more marked and blue rings appear under the eyes. In old age the amount of fat is very low and the eyes are set deeply in their sockets. They also lose their sparkle, the skin on the brow bone is limp and forms a furrow in the outer corner of the eye. The vicinity of the eyes is heavily lined.

To achieve an impression of an old and sunken eye, brown or grey shadows are applied within the eye-socket near the bridge of the nose. Shadows are also applied on the upper eyelid. The furrow on the upper eyelid is made obvious by applying light make-up close to the brows, starting in the middle of the lid and passing transversly down towards the outer corner. Wrinkles and lines are applied as described in the following chapter. Light-coloured instead of dark eyelash make-up is applied. Very marked eyebrows brushed downward at the outer corners of the eyes make the eyes seem deeply set.

In cases where the required changes cannot be achieved by applying shadows, various plastic accessories should be used, such as foamed latex pieces or plastic pastes, putty, etc.

6.1.6.1. *The eyes of a drunkard.*
The eyes of a drunkard are usually dim, protruding and swollen, because the congested arteries increase the size of the fatty pads in the eye sockets.

The impression of the bloodshot eye of a drunkard is achieved by applying highlights on the upper and lower eye lids. The lower lid is also lined red close to the lashes. A sleepy, expressionless eye is achieved by applying a very light liner close to the lashes, which can also be made up in light tones.

6.1.7. *The White of the Eye*

To achieve larger eyes, the white of the eye is made more obvious by lining the edge of the lower lid with a white eye-liner. The line is drawn between the eye and lashes. The lid must be turned slightly outwards and the white make-up is applied with a very fine, flat brush. The upper lid is never made up in this way, because the lashes would conceal the white line. This method is very difficult and the make-up must be applied most carefully and gently. It is commonly used in negro masks.

6.1.8. *Atropine*

Atropine drops in the eye dilate the pupil which is then very marked. Atropine is very seldom used, only when madness or another mental disease should be portrayed. The pupil is very large and almost rigid and the sight is very blurred. Atropine should be applied solely by a physician.

6.2. THE NOSE

The nose is such a prominent feature of the face that even a slight change in its shape may alter the appearance of the entire face. In no case must the make-up man change the proportions of the face so that the final result would cause disharmony between the shape of the nose and the rest of the face. All changes must therefore look natural with the exception of fantastic, fairy-tale and clown's masks where exaggeration of a certain feature may bring the desired effect of the unreal or the supernatural.

Earlier, especially in the theatre, very light shadows were applied on the bridge of the nose and red–brown or grey–blue shadows were applied on the nostrils to make the nose seem very narrow.

Present make-up, however, abandoned this fashion because it is strongly affected by the more intensive lighting and by the more sensitive emulsions. Both these factors would ruthlessly disclose the unnatural appearance of a face made up in this way. The colours of the shadows must harmonize with the colour of the foundation make-up, and must imperceptibly blend into the skin.

Carefully and skilfully applied shadows and contrasts, backed by suitable lighting, may make a nose seem straighter, broader, shorter, or longer than it really is. An impression of a nose disfiguration can also be achieved (Fig. 37).

The distance between the eyes may be changed by suitable application of shadows and contrasts on the bridge of the nose. When plastic changes

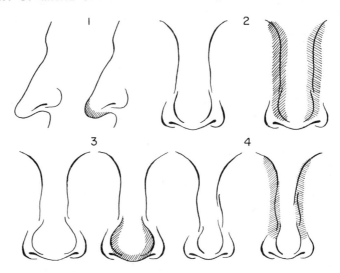

FIG. 37. Changes of nose shape achieved by contouring. 1. A shortened tip of the nose. 2. A narrowed nose achieved by the application of shadows to the sides of the nose. 3. A narrowed tip of the nose. 4. A corrected disfiguration of the nose achieved by contouring.

of the bridge of the nose take place, the position of the eyes changes most markedly. If the bridge of the nose is made higher the eyes appear very deep set. A broad bridge of the nose makes the eyes seem close.

The following paragraphs deal with the changes in nose shapes that may be achieved by the suitable application of contrasts and shadows, without the help of plastic pastes, nose putties or foamed latex accessories.

6.2.1. *Shadows and Highlights*

A broad nose is made narrower by applying shadows on its sides starting at the bridge of the nose downward towards the nostrils. The colour of the shades must blend with the colour of the eye shades.

A nose too broad at the roof, or a flat nose with a concave bridge, is narrowed by applying shadows only in the broad places. The same method is applied for noses with nostrils which are too broad or with a bulbous tip.

Eyes that are too wide apart may seem closer after shadowing the bridge of the nose (Figs. 38 and 39).

In the case of irregular and disfigured noses shadows are applied only on the most prominent parts. On the other side of the irregularity highlight is applied. The disfiguration is enhanced by applying highlights on the prominent part, and the shadows on the opposite side.

A slightly hooked nose is achieved by applying light make-up at the bridge and blending it down to the tip. Light-coloured make-up for

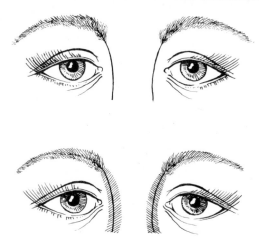

FIG. 38. A narrowed root of the nose achieved by the application of shadows.

enhacing larger areas is applied very carefully as this reflects light more strongly than the other colours (Figs. 40–45).

The ruddy or coarse texture of the nose for character make-up is achieved by red or red–brown make-up applied in tiny dots on a lighter foundation so that the colour spots appear as coarse skin. Red make-up is applied either with the finger-tips or with a coarse sponge by light patting. Broken veins can be achieved by the same technique.

Small nostrils are corrected by a light touch of red make-up. Big nostrils seem smaller when lighter toned make-up is applied.

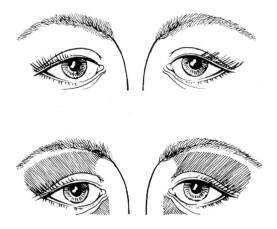

FIG. 39. A broadened root of the nose achieved by the application of highlights.

73

FIGS. 40–45. CONTOURING OF THE NOSE

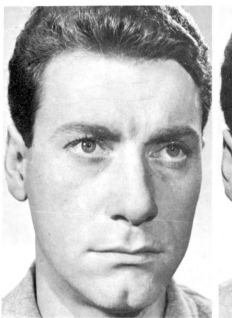

FIG. 40. Natural appearance of the actor.

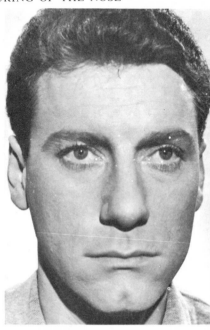

FIG. 41. A narrowed nose.

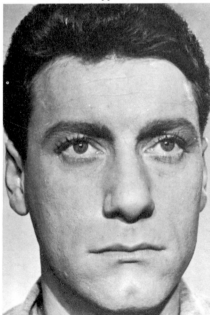

FIG. 42. A shortened nose.

FIG. 43. The nose is shortened and broadened.

FIG. 44. A face without make-up.

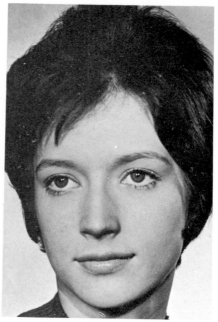

FIG. 45. The tip of the nose is shortened by shadowing.

6.3. THE LIPS

The lips and the eyes are the most important features of the face. They must be made up most carefully, especially in film and television. Wrong shape of the lips, wrong colour of the lipstick or an exaggerated outline of the lips has a damaging effect on the entire make-up. If it is not absolutely necessary to alter the character of the face by changing the shape of the lips, the make-up artist tries to maintain their natural outline or corrects them only very slightly (Figs. 46–51).

The lips may be enhanced; broad mouth and full lips are usually suppressed. The lips should look natural and fresh and lipstick is therefore applied only very thinly. Before lipstick is applied, the lips must be free from any make-up or powder. However, it is sometimes better to outline the lips before powdering the make-up, because flaws can easily be corrected on a fatty base. Some types of lips are plastically contoured. Such lips need not be enhanced and lipstick is applied very sparingly. The same applies to protruding lips. A broad mouth and lips that are too full are narrowed by applying foundation make-up in the corners of the mouth and on the edges of the lips. This must not be exaggerated beyond a certain limit, as lip movement would betray this very quickly. If thin

75

FIGS. 46–48. MAKE-UP OF THE LIPS

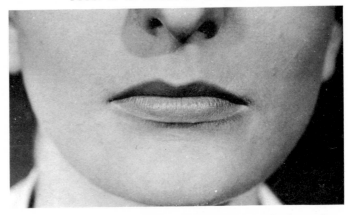

FIG. 46. Made-up lips with natural line maintained.

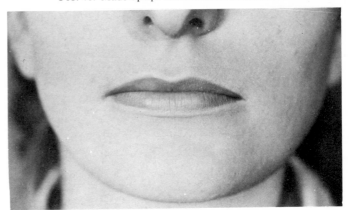

FIG. 47. Narrowed lips.

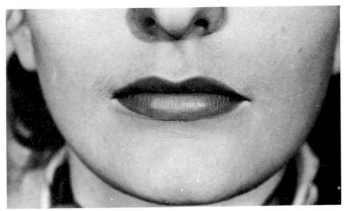

FIG. 48. Broadened lips.

FIGS. 49–51. VARIOUS LIP SHADES.

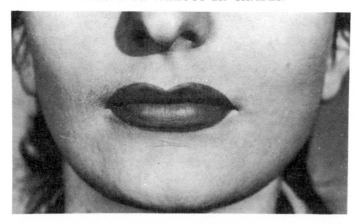

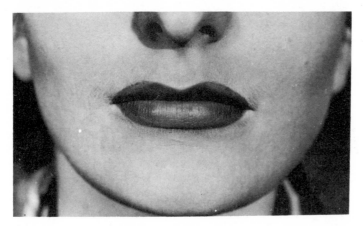

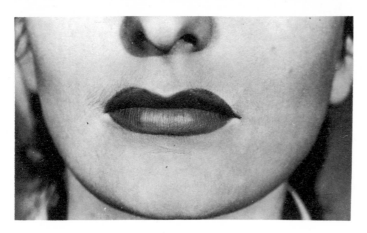

lips are made fuller, high arches starting from the corner of the mouth should never be painted because the lips do not look natural. Thin lips should be painted only slightly broader than their natural shape. The outline of the lower lip should remain natural and in proportion to the upper lip. The outlines of the upper and lower lip should converge to the same points in the outer corners of the mouth. The upper lip line should be turned slightly upwards in drooping corners to give the mouth a smiling appearance.

The desired contour of the lips is marked with a lip-liner or a small brush. The mouth is shut, but the lips are not pressed together. Lipstick is then applied on the entire surface of the lips including the area which is seen when the mouth is open. Lipstick is applied from the centre of the upper lip to the corners of the mouth. When applied to the upper lip, the lips are pressed slightly together to blot the excess lipstick on the lower lip. The lipstick is allowed to dry for a few moments and then the lips are lightly powdered. Lipstick is thus fixed and makes a good base for a final, very subtle, touch of lipstick, or cream rouge which is applied with a fine, flat brush (Fig. 52).

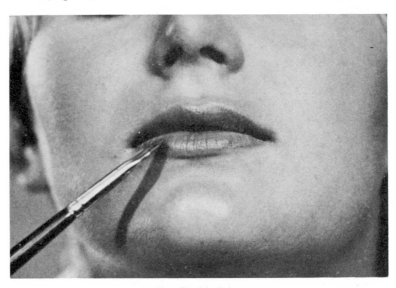

FIG. 52. Lip lining.

Dark red lipstick or rouges are never used; medium or light tones of red are preferred. Dark red liners should be used only in big theatres to enhance the contour of the lips. For make-up of children and for young, fair-haired girls only pastel-toned lipsticks are used. Some light lipsticks are, however, apt to darken. This is prevented by applying skin-coloured lipstick, the surplus of which is removed by tissuing off and then the required, pastel-toned lipstick is applied; orange tones are never used because they look very unnatural.

Men's lips are almost never made up; if necessary, natural-coloured lipstick is used very sparingly on the lips of very young characters. The contour of men's lips is never lined. On too fresh-looking lips of older characters a bluish make-up is lightly applied to subdue the natural red colour of the lips. The same applies to older women.

For old age make-up, tiny lines are drawn in the foundation on the lips and their immediate vicinity. For older, peasant women make-up, lips are made up in natural tones corresponding to the coloration of their own lips.

6.4. CHEEK ROUGE

Cheek rouge is a very important factor in film and theatre make-up. It gives the face a fresh look and helps to model the contours in certain type of lighting, providing it is correctly applied (Fig. 53).

Dry or cream rouge is applied most frequently on high cheek bones and carefully blended in all directions. In oval faces, rouge is applied on the lightest point of the cheek bones and is blended in all directions, mainly towards the temple. It should not get too near to the nose and eyes. The

FIG. 53. The application of cheek rouge. 1. To the round face. 2. To the tri-angular face. 3. To the oblong face.

same applies to high cheek bones. In narrow faces rouge is applied to the centre of the cheek bone and is blended on a small area towards the temple. Rouge is applied near the nose of broad faces which then appear narrower. A light touch of red may make too prominent a chin also appear smaller (Fig. 54).

FIG. 54. Face narrowed by the application of rouge to the cheeks.

Cheek rouge may be applied more generously for big stages. Care must be taken, however, in smaller theatres and in colour film in order not to exaggerate the application, as the desired natural appearance would be definitely distorted. In make-up for monochromatic film a little red shading may also be used.

6.5. THE FINGERNAILS

Make-up should always be completed by well-manicured hands with well-shaped fingernails, polished with matching lacquer.

The make-up man should always make sure that the colour of the finger-nails corresponds to the colour of the lipstick. If not, the hands may be rapidly manicured in the following way.

To soften the polish a wad of cotton wool moistened with lacquer re-mover is lightly pressed to all fingernails successively. The softened polish is then easily wiped off with the wad slightly moistened with the lacquer remover. The nails are carefully filed maintaining their natural shape. A good, nourishing cream is applied to the nail beds to supply the cuticle with fat and moisture. The cuticle is then gently pushed back with a smooth wooden rod. The nourishing cream must then be removed because the polish would not hold to the greasy fingernail. Polish in the colour matching that of the lipstick is then applied with a small brush. Some manufacturers produce and supply the so-called "primer" for application to the fingernail under the lacquer.

80

Bottles containing nailpolish must be well shaken before use, because pigments usually settle at the bottom. The first coat of the polish is applied in one stroke to the middle of the fingernail. When dry, a second layer is applied, thus covering the fingernail completely; if polish with a pearly finish is used a third coating is usually necessary. The polish is then allowed to dry and harden properly.

6.6.   MAKE-UP FOR MEN

Make-up for men must always appear entirely natural. Foundations are of darker tones than those for women, but contour blending is done by the same technique as for women. It is sometimes advisable to shadow the ears because they are not concealed by the hair and reflect light too much. Lines and wrinkles are not removed, except when the actor portrays a character, whose life-story begins in early youth.

6.6.1. *Beard*

A clean-shaven face, a dark beard area or an unshaven face help to illustrate a character. A darker beard area gives the younger actor a more virile appearance, whereas a concealed beard area of an older actor gives him a younger look.

The beard area is not regularly concealed in present make-up for men in colour film. In television and monochromatic film, however, it is advisable to use a beard stick to make-up the beard area because otherwise the

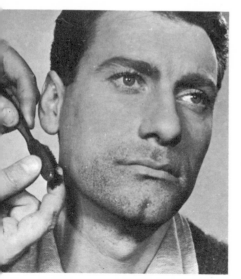

Figs. 55 and 56.   An unshaven face achieved by sprinkling with mascara.

face would look unshaven. For coloured film and theatre make-up it is usually sufficient to use foundation make-up. For dark-haired men, however, the beard is enhanced by grey–blue shadowing, giving the face a manly appearance.

The appearance of an unshaven face is achieved by spraying the beard area with mascara of various tints of brown; either water-resistant or water-soluble mascara may be used for this purpose. The mascara is applied to a toothbrush and sprinkled onto the beard area in tiny droplets. To gain a more plastic impression white mascara is applied in the same way to the beard area of older characters. For white-haired men only white mascara is used (Figs. 55 and 56).

A make-up pencil or an eye-liner of suitable colour may also be used to draw a hint of a moustache on the upper lip of adolescent boys.

6.6.2. The Eyebrows.

The eyebrows of men thicken with age and are usually darker than the hair. The shape of the eyebrows should also correspond to the type of character presented. It is usually sufficient to draw it with an eyebrow pencil. Deep-set eyes may be achieved by brushing the eyebrows down, whereas the eyes seem to be larger when the brows are brushed upwards. Men's eyebrows are not plucked but the part that is to be concealed is stuck to the skin with a thin layer of soap and the resulting smooth area is carefully made up with the foundation and powder. It is then shaded in the required tones of auxiliary make-up and is powdered again. The new eyebrows are either drawn with an eyebrow pencil or false eyebrows are used.

6.6.3. The Hair

The hair of middle-aged men is thinning, the forehead is usually getting longer and a bald spot appears on the crown of the head. In some cases the hairline does not change too much but the skin of the head is seen through the thinning hair. It is possible to achieve an impression of unchanged hairline by using a dark liner and tinting the hair with mascara. The lining must not be done too crudely and the colour of the liner and mascara should be a shade lighter than the natural colour of the hair. Too high or too prominent a forehead is shaded and the shadows are blended towards the hair and down to the eyebrows. This also helps to subdue the reflection of light (Figs. 57–59).

6.6.4. The Jaws

It is best to apply pancake shadows with a moist sponge to the upper and lower jaws. For small areas a brush may be used.

All pancake shadows are applied on a clean, dry face, free of make-up

FIGS. 57–59. AN ALTERED HAIRLINE

FIG. 57. The natural area of the hairline.

FIGS. 58 and 59. The hairline is altered with the eyebrow make-up pencil and/or with mascara.

and grease. Pancake foundation is applied to the entire face, concealing the shadows previously applied. Pancake highlights are applied under the eyes with a wet brush, and in the lines around the mouth and nose. When pancake is completely dry the entire face is powdered, the surplus being removed with a powder brush. The areas that were shadowed are carefully rubbed with the fingers, to emphasize the amount of shadow desired. The effect is judged in the mirror (Figs. 60 and 61).

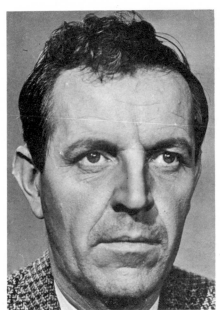

FIGS. 60 and 61. An impression of a thinner or rounder face achieved by the application of shadows.

If a fatty foundation is used, the shadows should be applied over the foundation. The foundation is applied on the face either with the fingers or with a moist sponge to achieve an even, smooth layer of make-up. Shadows are applied with the finger-tips or a small brush.

7. CORRECTIVE MAKE-UP

CORRECTIVE make-up is used to achieve various changes in the appearance, expression and character of the actor's face. It is mainly used when the actor has to portray an authentic person or if the dramatist's conception of a certain character requires it. Corrective make-up is the most difficult part of the make-up artist's work. He must use all his artistic imagination, knowledge, and experience. He must also co-operate closely with the actor, the producer, the lighting man, and the camera operator.

Before the make-up artist starts, he has to study the film or television scenario or the play very thoroughly and he must analyse the particular roles most carefully. He has to find out all the important factors that may affect the expression and features of the actor's face, such as living conditions, profession, social standing, hobbies, life experience, disposition, emotional life, health, etc., so that he can create a mask which faithfully illustrates the effects life has upon that human face.

Characteristic make-up and masks indicating a villain, a comedian, a bad or a good character, are not used any more. The actor must create the particular character of the play or film, after a thorough study and minute analysis of the part. The make-up man helps him to achieve and maintain throughout filming or performance, all the typical features of the character he represents—his age, race, profession and other significant factors that may have a bearing upon the appearance of the character portrayed.

Corrective make-up is used when some changes of the face are to be achieved, for example a broad jaw is to be made narrower or high cheek-bones are to be made less obvious, etc.

The purpose of normal make-up is to improve the physical charm of the performers, to conceal blemishes of the complexion, to overcome the effects of strong illumination and to level the difference between the sensitivity of the human eye and the film negatives to colours, whereas corrective make-up not only maintains but emphasizes some cosmetic defects such as ageing of the skin, lines, wrinkles, etc. Corrective make-up requires a real artist with a refined taste and a sense of proportion who has a deep knowledge of the physiological changes of the skin characteristics for a certain age. He must, of course, skilfully master the technique of make-up.

85

7.1. MAKE-UP FOR MIDDLE AGE

Between 30 and 50 years of age the first typical signs of ageing appear in the features of almost all people. The development of these signs depends on the physical type, the way of life and on health.

People who have spent most of their lives in the open air have ruddy faces, whereas the complexion of those who chiefly keep indoors acquires a greyish–yellow tint. Healthy people usually maintain their fresh appearance longer. Others who suffer from an illness have abnormally coloured complexions, either very pale or very red, sometimes cyanotic, especially those suffering from high blood pressure or circulatory disorders.

Exercise in the open air and sports have favourable effects upon health but the early signs of ageing appear just the same. Tiny wrinkles appear in the outer corners of the eyes, on the forehead, throat, at the nostrils and around the mouth. These ridges deepen in the course of years.

Slim, hard-working people and sportsmen usually have sharper and more prominent features with slightly hollow cheeks and high cheek bones. This is the result of physical strain which prevents fat from depositing under the skin. The hair is getting grey and is thinning, the hairline of men recedes and bald spots appear on the crown of their heads. Fat people often acquire rounder features, because fat settles in their cheeks, chin and at the back of their neck.

The eyebrows and eyelashes of women are thinner, whereas men's eyebrows grow thicker and are greying. The face usually maintains this changed appearance for a number of years within the period of middle age.

As a rule, the physical appearance of the actors and actresses is the determining factor for the parts that suit them best.

Corrective make-up is most often used to achieve a younger appearance. Many women's make-up calls for some change of age towards youth, because certain parts require younger looking performers.

Film and television cameras are more sensitive to any change in make-up than the audience in the theatre, and therefore film and television make-up must be done very carefully when convincing changes of age are to be achieved. The cameraman in the film studio may use diffusion lenses, filters and softer, flattering illumination and thus helps the make-up artist to reduce the age of the performers. This, however, is rarely done for men, as lines and wrinkles in men's faces add virility and emphasize the character.

In the theatre the distance between the stage and the audience enables one to use make-up of more vivid colours and deeper contouring which together with the distance, helps to conceal minor complexion defects caused by age.

The typical signs of middle age are wrinkles around the eyes and mouth, and on the throat. Make-up for this life-period can be almost always accomplished without the use of plastic accessories. However, wrinkles should not be too emphasized. It is advisable to stress other signs of middle age, such as the changing colour of the hair, the receding hairline, etc. Highlights and shadows must be applied very carefully to the face and must blend well with the foundation make-up so that there is no defined line of colour.

In some cases, middle age may be emphasized by using make-up very sparingly or by not using it at all. Sometimes, when the areas around the mouth and eyes are not made up, the face looks older. Without foundation make-up, all wrinkles, furrows and natural highlights in the face are very obvious; they may be even more enhanced by applying more shadows to the face. Without make-up the eyes lack lustre and without lipstick the lips are not clearly outlined. This technique is used when a middle-aged actor plays a part corresponding to his own age (Figs. 62–66).

If it is necessary to increase the actor's age, it is advisable to stress the furrows and ridges by applying soft shadows to the face with a brush or with the finger-tips. Fine, but well-marked, wrinkles can be drawn with a sharp grey eyebrow pencil. Black pencils are never used because the lines look too hard and unnatural.

Wrinkles, furrows or shadows should not be applied without a deep knowledge of the function, position and location of the most important facial muscles. The actor's face, his smile, laugh and way of speech are the best guides to the make-up artist for determining which parts of the face become more prominent and which appear flat. This helps him to decide where the highlights and shadows should be applied.

To emphasize shadows and highlights of the face, darker toned auxiliary make-up is applied to the furrows and ridges and lighter make-up to the prominent parts of the face, but care should be taken not to stress the latter too much. Wrinkles and furrows are traced and shadows are applied before the face is powdered. The whole auxiliary make-up should be expertly blended into the foundation make-up.

If fatty foundation is used all shadows and highlights as well as lines and wrinkles are applied on the foundation make-up, whereas with pancake shadows and highlights are applied to the skin, which should be free from grease, oil or previous make-up. A sponge is best for applying pancake shadows to large areas such as the jaw; for smaller areas a brush may be used. Pancake foundation is then applied on the entire face concealing the shadows and highlights. When it is completely dry the surplus is removed with a powder brush. The dried pancake can also be powdered first and then brushed with a powder brush. The areas on which highlights were applied are carefully rubbed with the fingers so as to emphasize only the required amount of shadow or highlight. The effect should first be judged by looking into the mirror held at arm's length. In order to photograph well the shadows should be barely visible, more marked ones are too exaggerated on the screen. If dry rouge is added to the cheeks it must be applied very lightly, so as not to damage the finished make-up. Invisible fatty foundation cream should be rubbed into very dry skin before pancake is applied.

If fatty foundation is used, shadows and highlights are applied by patting and not by strokes, because the even surface of the foundation would be

FIGS. 62–66. GRADUAL AGEING ACHIEVED BY CHARACTER MAKE-UP WITHOUT THE USE OF ACCESSORIES

FIG. 62.   A face without make-up.

FIG. 63. A face with applied make-up.

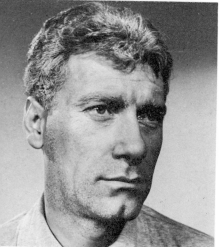

FIGS. 64 and 65. Make-up for middle age — a basic knowledge of the facial anatomy is necessary.

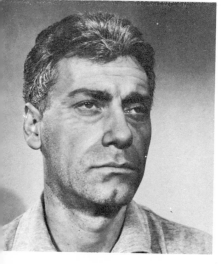

FIG. 66. Theatre make-up for advanced age.

damaged. The area around the eyes and the furrows around the mouth and nose may be enhanced by pancake carefully blended with the foundation by patting. Wrinkles and shadows can also be painted on the skin when emulsion or transparent make-up is used. These types of make-up blend the shadows with the complexion so well that the final result appears quite natural. Deeper ridges can be achieved by drawing them on the skin exactly in the places where they actually appear. It is advisable to pucker the face to see where the furrows actually are and then enhance them slightly with the auxiliary make-up. Ridges, lines and furrows should never be traced in places where they would normally never appear.

Coarse or ruddy complexion is achieved in the manner described in detail in Chapter 6.

7.2. MAKE-UP FOR OLDER AGE

To achieve the impression of older age, all ridges, furrows, shadows and highlights must be more enhanced. In the theatre, the make-up man may obtain good results with nose putty in making certain plastic changes on the skin, whereas foam rubber pieces have to be used in film and television when a heavy character make-up is to be convincing on the screen.

In older age the face reflects life much more intensely than in middle age. Ridges and furrows are in the same places but are much pronounced and much deeper. In older age all parts of the body undergo certain changes, that have, however, one characteristic feature in common — gradual atrophy of almost all parts and organs of the body.

7.2.1. *The Skin*

The skin of the face, throat, arms and hands changes most. It loses its elasticity, gets thinner, and more pigment deposits in it causing a yellowish-brown tint, especially in the areas that are not covered by clothes. On the forehead, temples, lips and on the backs of the hands there appear yellow marks which gradually darken to a brownish tone. Weaker activity of the heart causes cyanosis of the lips. The amount of fat is reduced in the subcutaneous tissue, the fatty pads diminish and the skin seems loose. The facial bones, such as jaw and chin covered with thin skin, become more prominent. The loss of fat and elasticity causes wrinkling of the skin and the formation of deep ridges and furrows. The furrows at the outer corners of the eyes get more pronounced, on the forehead there appear lateral ridges and at the bridge of the nose vertical ones can be observed. The ridges around the mouth and nose deeper when the lips sink in the toothless mouth. The skin on the hands is thin and dry.

7.2.2. *The Hair*

Hair loses its lustre and pigment and often falls out. Grey and white hair is typical for older age. Men usually have bald spots on the crown of the head and the skin there is shiny; tough hairs grow in the nostrils and ears. On the upper lips and chins of old women hairs also appear. The finger-nails are thick, lustreless, bluish-grey or yellow.

7.2.3. *The Eye*

The eyes and their surrounding parts change very much with age. The amount of fat in the eye-socket decreases, the eyes are deep sunken and the brow bones are very marked. The cheek bones which in youth were imperceptible in the rounded face, are very prominent in old age because the fatty pads in the cheeks are missing. The depression on the temples seem deeper too.

The upper lid loses its elasticity and droops over the eye by its own weight, giving it a tired look. The skin of the eyelids forms pouches, and is of bluish or brownish colour. The white of the eye is stained yellow by the fat deposited under the conjunctiva. The cornea is lustreless and the pupil is small.

7.2.3.1. *Eye make-up.*

One of the most important features in make-up for older age are the eyes. In most cases they seem to be sunken. Shadows are therefore applied more heavily on the sides of the nose and within the eye-sockets in the inner corner of the eyes near the upper lids. Very natural looking furrows and bags under eyes may be made with the help of a special plastic paste.

Heavy pouches should be made of foamed latex. The rubber piece should be fixed near the lower line of the eyelashes and should reach to the edge of the eyesocket. Plastic accessories may also be used for shaping the skin ridges on the upper lids that reach from the middle of the lid diagonally down to the corner of the eye. It may also be achieved by heavily applied highlights. The colour of the eyelashes may be changed with white or grey mascara.

7.2.4. *Shadows and Highlights*

Shadows and highlights are applied by the same technique as for middle-age make-up, but much more generously. Sometimes, however, it is necessary to use a foamed latex cast to cover the entire face and thus conceal the young features of the actor. Lipstick is used very sparingly for monochrome. For coloured film a little blue is sometimes applied on the lips to subdue their fresh, young-looking red colour. Rouge for the cheeks is used very seldom. Sometimes reddish or red-brown make-up is used to characterize the types of people who live in the open air most of their lives.

When an impression of very old skin is to be achieved and foamed latex casts are not available, it is possible to cover the area where most furrows appear—or the entire face, if necessary—with a plastic paste mixed with foundation make-up in a layer of required thickness. The furrows and ridges may be traced very easily in this layer with a sharp modelling tool, lengthwise and crosswise to achieve an impression of especially dry and furrowed skin. If make-up must be powdered, it is advisable to pat the made-up, powdered areas with a sponge moistened with transparent make-up to eliminate a matt finish that would photograph flat. This kind of make-up for old age is used in film for short filming periods only.

Powder in the character make-up is used only as a fixing agent, or for concealing shine caused by fatty or emulsion foundation make-up. Powder is almost never used on transparent make-up.

7.2.5. The Throat

Corrective make-up must also include make-up of the visible part of the throat. In old age the throat gets either thin and wrinkled or fat with a more or less marked double chin. Both effects may be achieved by clever application of shadows and highlights. Horizontal furrows and ridges are drawn by sharp pencils, vertical shadows and highlights are usually more flat, and are applied with blending brushes or with the finger-tips. In more exact cases the double-chin folds are made of foamed latex casts.

7.2.6. The Arms and Hands

Suitably made-up hands and arms complete the character make-up. Sometimes the arms and hands must bear the signs of profession and age, whereas for normal make-up, colour rendering is satisfactory. The impression of bony hands and arms with prominent veins is achieved by straight application of shadows and highlights on the clean, dry hands and arms, free from any make-up, so that the areas without make-up appear as bones and veins. Make-up of lighter shade is applied to them making them even more prominent. The process is completed by the application of transparent make-up. Veins which are too pale must be outlined in blue. They are located by submerging the arms and hands in warm water and then shaking them for a few minutes; the veins become more apparent and their course may be enhanced by blue colour. Otherwise close-ups of raised arms would instantly betray the youth and freshness of the skin (Figs. 67–69).

Dark colour must be applied on the finger-nails of actors representing hard-working characters. The furrows on the joints of the fingers must also be made more apparent.

FIGS. 67–69. AGEING OF THE HANDS

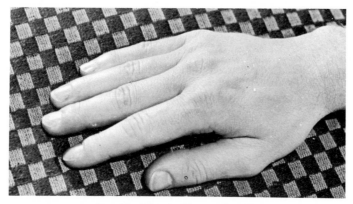

FIG. 67. A hand without make-up.

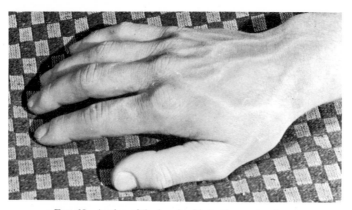

FIG. 68. Ageing of the hand achieved by contouring.

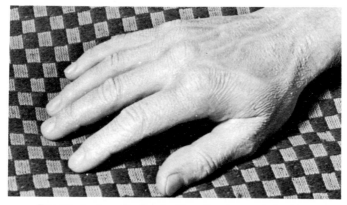

FIG. 69. Ageing of the hand achieved by the use of plastic paste.

93

7.2.7 Gradual Ageing

If the play or scenario covers a long period of time, actors chosen for the parts must be of a type which allows the make-up man to alter their age in both directions. The possibility of diminishing age is most important as it is always more difficult to decrease age than to increase it.

In this particularly difficult section of the character make-up, the make-up man must take great care not to stress too much any age period of the role, as he would necessarily limit the possibilities of make-up of the remaining epochs. He usually starts with normal make-up and, as the first signs of ageing, stresses all the natural furrows and ridges, or applies grey to the hair. Gradually he uses heavier shadows and highlights. Then he adds grey hair accessories, or changes the wig, especially for women. Then he stresses the furrows around the eyes. In this prudent way good results are achieved in most cases. Sometimes it is also possible to make up the actor for middle age and gradually sponge off the furrows and other signs of age. In the end additional ridges and pouches may be added for the older age.

Each make-up, however, must be treated individually. The signs of old age are not the same in all people and cannot be created in a uniform way.

7.2.8. Rapid Ageing

Rapid ageing is one of the extreme make-up effects that can be successfully achieved only in film, with the help of a series of fade-outs. The actor remains in a fixed position during shooting and signs of increasing age are gradually added in his face and each shot of the altered make-up lasts only a few frames. Hair pieces and plastic accessories are also added in the same way. All shots are then joined and the actor ages rapidly in a few seconds in front of the audience.

In television, however, this effect can be achieved only rarely under extraordinarily favourable conditions and then the mask is so simple that it may be changed within the few seconds of camera change. In the theatre, however, the effect of rapid ageing cannot be achieved at all.

7.2.9. Very Old Age

Sometimes a part requires an extraordinarily old character, of 80 or more years. If the actor himself is old his own furrows and ridges may be stressed to achieve the right result. Otherwise it is necessary to use a latex mask covering the entire face.

7.3. OBESITY

The impression of obesity is achieved by the application of lighter make-up on the cheeks, under the chin and on the jaw. Shadows are ap-

94

plied on the natural folds of the skin. In colour film and in the theatre vivid red is applied on the cheeks. The centre of the face should be a shade lighter to enhance the impression of a fat face. Rouge is applied at the highest spot of the facial muscle along the nasolabial ridge, but not too near to it. A lighter area between the ridge and the red spot makes the muscle seem higher and more pudgy. Rouge is blended well so as not to make a sharp colour line.

7.4 SLIMNESS

Slimness may be enhanced by repeated application of light make-up. This is applied by patting as strokes could damage the powdered areas. This make-up gives a natural shine to the prominent parts of the face, for example to the high cheek bones.

7.5. COLOUR CHANGE OF THE COMPLEXION

An actor can appear to change from a white man to a coloured one and vice versa by means of suitable make-up and lighting. This can be done especially well on the stage. Carmine make-up is applied to the face, hands and other uncovered parts of the body. When lit by green mono-chromatic light the make-up appears dark brown. When the light is changed to red, there is nothing to suggest the presence of the make-up as it is of the same colour as the lighting and the actor appears as white.

Character lines can be created by carmine make-up by variations of depth and a young man may age by a change of lighting. This technique may be used to achieve other effects as well, such as changes in the facial expression, when a benevolent face can change into a diabolical looking character, or changes in the colour of dress, etc., by merely switching on different lights.

7.6. SKIN FIXATION

For some parts it is necessary to change the actor's age over a wide range of time. Such roles should be played by middle-aged actors whose types permit a decrease in age, which is always more difficult to achieve than an increase.

The age of an expressive face can be changed relatively easily in both directions with a suitable make-up. To achieve old age all natural wrinkles and furrows can be stressed with a suitable make-up or with the help of foamed latex make-up accessories.

When the face is to appear younger it is sometimes necessary to fix weak muscles and smoothen the actor's complexion. If the actor wears a wig it is usually sufficient to lift the skin of the face at the sides with two strips of fine gauze or muslin. The ends of the strips are gummed firmly to the spot from where the skin is to be lifted and the loose ends are tied under the wig. It is possible to lift up the skin of the cheeks and the eye area by drawing it up at the temples. The faded skin of the throat, mouth and double chin may be lifted up in this way by attaching the strips just under the ears at the lower jaw and drawing the skin up and back. The loose ends are tied at the nape of the neck (Fig. 70).

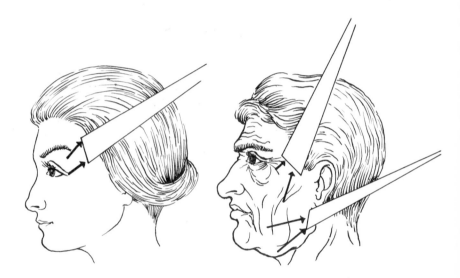

FIG. 70. Uplifting of limp skin.

The gauze is carefully made up in the same way and colour as the complexion of the face. The wig is then set firmly on the head and well gummed.

7.6.1. *The Mongolian Eye*

The Mongolian eye can be imitated in the same way as skin fixation.

The inner corner of the Mongolian eye is partly covered with the skin duplication of the upper lid. The lower lid is short and the edge line is parallel with the line of the upper lid. The strips of gauze are glued to the temples at the hairline and are drawn above the ears to the back of the head where they are firmly tied together. A securely fitted wig helps to hold the lifted skin in such a way that the shape of the slanting eye remains unchanged. The dark lining of the upper lid starts at the lowest point of the inner corner, and near the line of the eyelashes to the outer corner of the eye and is slightly lengthened upward. The dark lining of the lower lid starts approximately in the centre of the lid and is parallel to the line of the upper lid. The line of the eyebrow is adapted to the newly made eye-line.

7.7. OTHER POSSIBILITIES OF CORRECTIVE MAKE-UP

It is possible to alter the actor's appearance, or his age, with normal or corrective make-up, with a suitable wig or various hair pieces supposing that the type of the actor's face and age approximately correspond to the required changes.

Sometimes, however, it is necessary to alter the shape of some part of the face or of the face as a whole, if the actor is to represent an entirely different type and age, especially if he is to create a historic, fantastic or fairy-tale character.

Before foam latex accessories were known, various modelling materials, such as nose putty, plastic pastes, collodion, cotton wool, and various kinds of fine fabric, etc., were used. These materials are in use even nowadays, especially when the use of latex pieces is not economical or if the conditions for their preparation are not favourable.

It is easy to achieve good results with the help of the above mentioned materials only on the bony parts of the face or on those that are not strained mechanically, for example on the nose, chin, brow, some parts of the forehead and cheek bones. On soft and furrowed parts of the face, however, these materials crack and separate at the edges due to the movement of the muscles. Good results are obtained in these cases with the use of foam latex make-up accessories.

Special make-up effects are very difficult to achieve and they represent the summit of the art of make-up. Every make-up artist should carefully balance and consider all possibilities before he starts work, so that the result should adequately reflect his efforts.

7.7.1. *Nose Putty*

Nose putties are usually rather thick mixtures of waxes and resins and are used for minor changes of the bony parts of the face, especially nose and chin. A small piece of this material is moulded in the fingers until warmth and slight pressure soften it sufficiently to become pliable. Nose putty must be able to stick to the face without any adhesive. It should be tinted pink or various shades of red.

7.7.2. *Plastic Pastes*

Plastic pastes are mixtures of natural and synthetic waxes and are considerably softer than nose putties. They are sticky and elastic and can therefore be used on the soft parts of the face. Various furrows, scars, pouches under the eyes and other minor skin defects can be modelled, as well as concealed, with their help. Sometimes they are combined with foundation grease so that they blend with other made-up parts of the face.

7.7.2.1. *Procedure.* The parts on which the pastes and putties are going to be modelled have to be carefully cleaned. First of all, every trace of fat must be removed. The modelling material adheres much better to carefully cleaned skin. Sometimes a thin layer of spirit gum is applied to the modelled area beforehand as it prevents the material from falling off the skin of the face when the actor perspires. If the material sticks to the fingers too much while modelling it is advisable to moisten it a little with water or smear it with *Vaseline.* Fatty foundation make-up can be used which gives the modelling material a similar colour tint to that of the other made-up parts of the face. The imperceptible blending of the modelled parts with the skin is most important for good results. The surface of the modelled parts can be smoothed by very gentle strokes of a slightly warmed modelling spatula.

7.7.2.2. *The nose.* Putty or paste is most frequently used for changing the shape of the nose. It straightens a concave nasal bone, enlarges a small nose, broadens it or makes it bent, flat or deformed. If the nose is to be made higher a little cylinder is moulded in the fingers and is then laid lengthwise upon the nose, from the bridge down to the tip and the material is modelled to the required shape, taking care that it blends with the bridge, tip and both sides of the nose. A snub, round-tipped nose is made by attaching a small ball of modelling putty or a paste to the tip of the nose. Great care must be taken to blend it with the bridge of the nose and with both sides. Every modelling material should be stained pink or light red so that it resembles the colour of skin. Otherwise the modelled parts would be too pale with a greyish tint and would look too thick in the strong studio lights, as the putty and paste reflect the rays of the lamps more strongly than the skin. The modelled parts also have a rather different structure and porosity than the skin, and sometimes the addition looks lifeless when carelessly made up.

It is possible to broaden the nostrils—when foamed latex is not available—with the help of cork which is inserted into the nostrils. The cork pieces are obtainable in a variety of sizes, they have an aperture for breathing and their length can be easily adjusted as required.

Plastic pastes can be used for gumming loose strands of the beard by a special technique. It is a very convenient method for short and medium beards which are gummed on large areas. An entirely natural look of several days' growth of beard or of an unshaven face is easily achieved (Fig. 71).

Plastic pastes replace the formerly used spirit gum which caused troubles in these cases. Spirit gum glistens too much and the shine is

Fig. 71. Special use of the plastic paste. Sleekly combed hair is thinly covered with the plastic paste.

removed only with considerable difficulties; it is brittle and cracks. The solvents, usually ether, either pure or mixed with alcohol, irritate the skin. When this adhesive is used frequently under unfavourable working conditions (heat, dust), especially in film and television studios, eczema or dermatitis may develop.

Nose putty and plastic pastes may be prepared in the following way:

Nose Putty

Yellow beeswax	25 g
Colophony	15 g
Kaolin	12 g
Titanium dioxide	5 g
Vulcan red	

Plastic Paste

Plastic paste may be prepared by heating equal parts of white beeswax and powdered kaolin. The warm mixture is stirred until cool.

7.7.2.3. *Scars.* Scars, especially deep ones, are made by thick collodion on absolutely clean and degreased skin. The collodion is applied by one or two strokes of a medium-soft brush, carefully outlining the shape of the scar. When the scar is to be deeper a fine modelling spatula is used on the collodion layer and the neighbouring skin is furrowed into the required shape with the fingers. It is possible to deepen the scar by applying a second layer of collodion. Drying is accelerated by a stream of warm air from a hair-dryer (Figs. 72–76).

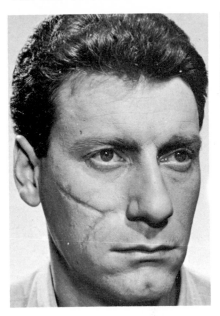
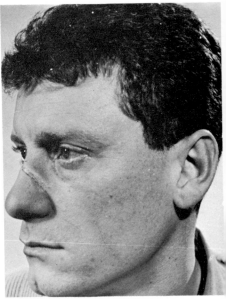

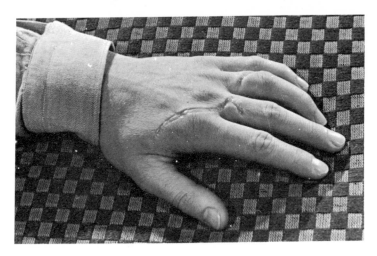

Figs. 72–74. Collodion scars.

The scars can be removed either by applying a new layer of collodion which dissolves the dried one or by organic solvents such as chloroform, ether, etc. Scars made of plastic pastes may be modelled on the actor's face without fear of irritating the skin.

The surface of a scar made of plastic paste can be either smooth and shiny, slightly wrinkled or can even imitate a deep plastic defor-

100

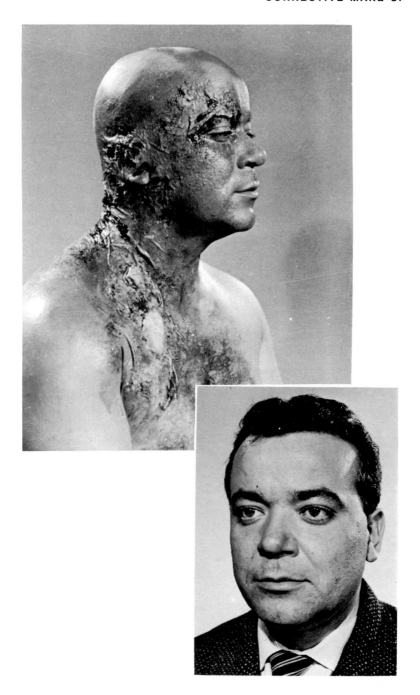

FIGS. 75 and 76. Collodion blisters and burns.

mation. Pastes have the great advantage that the structure of the edges can be more easily wrinkled than those made of collodion, where the character of the whole scar is identical and sometimes the lustre is too apparent and cannot easily be concealed. Plastic paste scars are, however, less resistant to mechanical damage.

A special variety of plastic pastes based on wax are the mixtures of plastic dispersions which are also very convenient for the make-up of scars. A suitably coloured dispersion is applied with a brush on well-stretched skin in as many layers as are needed to achieve the required shape and depth of the scar. The surface of the scar can be made up after the dispersion has dried. The dispersions dry within a few minutes through body temperature, adhere reliably to the skin, their surface is sufficiently porous, and they are very elastic.

7.7.3. *Teeth*

Teeth are also an important factor in the face of an actor representing a certain character. Today it is almost never necessary to conceal gold fillings as was necessary quite often in the past, because every actor tries to have perfect teeth nowadays. However, if a younger person is to play the part of an older character, it is necessary to adapt the teeth as well. Black tooth enamel, which was frequently used to create an impression of a missing tooth, is nowadays used only very rarely in film studios as strong light and close-ups betray this kind of make-up immediately. It is used only in the theatre. A more natural result is achieved by the use of white tooth enamel stained brown. The enamel is applied unevenly on the teeth which lose their sound appearance. If the actor has gaps in his teeth he can have this bridged with removable crowns. If a certain role requires a deformed set of teeth, it is best to have a complete dental palate made (Fig. 77).

7.7.4. *Use of Fish Vesicle*

Wrinkled skin and pouches under the eyes are imitated with the help of fish vesicles. A required shape corresponding to the whole area of the lower part of the eye-socket and narrowing to the eye-corners is cut from it. The bottom edge near the outer corner is unevenly cut, gummed in its place with spirit gum or rubber adhesive and made-up. A fine yet firm woven fabric can be used instead. The wrinkles are obtained by a layer of collodion or plastic paste. It is very difficult to fix the fish vesicle safely. It is too shiny and must be made-up very carefully — a tiresome process which demands great skill.

7.7.5. *Reinforced Laminated Accessories*

Reinforcing is a very convenient but often neglected method for

FIG. 77. A suitably-shaped dental palate completes the portrayal of a character.

making various irregularities and deformations of the head, back, etc. Various decorations, stage props and models for theatre and film studio use can be made by this technique.

7.7.5.1. *Procedure.* It is best to use uncoated paper dipped into liquid glue or starch solutions, and then place it into negative or positive plaster moulds. Positive moulds are used when a smooth surface is not absolutely necessary. The mould has to be carefully treated before the work is started, i.e. it must be ground or rubbed, polished and waxed or lubricated with a mixture of wax and *Vaseline* so that the paper does not stick to it.

Strips of paper of suitable size are dipped into the glue and are laid into the mould in as many layers as are required for the size, thickness and solidity of the final product. Usually three to five layers are sufficient, but bigger objects need more layers. To increase the solidity it is advisable to use fabric strips in combination with paper. Paper can be replaced by

103

fabric or cotton wool, or all these materials may be used in combination with each other.

Nowadays reinforced accessories for the make-up of cheeks and nose are rarely used in film and television studios; usually only on such occasions when their unnatural and often exaggerated look does not matter, for example for the make-up of clowns or comedians. Reinforced accessories have been replaced by foam latex products, especially in film and television studios. However, reinforced pieces are still the most convenient ones for small theatres, music-halls, minor shows, etc.

In more exact cases, especially when the actor's mimics must not be hampered by anything and his make-up has to be convincing and natural, foam latex products are being used more and more because their structure and porosity is very similar to that of skin.

8. MAKE-UP AND MAKE-UP IMPLEMENTS

THE make-up artist must know all kinds of make-up and aids for make-up so that he can make the most of them in his work. The choice of make-up at present is so varied in colour tones that the make-up artist need very seldom blend colours himself. He has to know, however, what kind and colour of make-up to choose with regard to the lighting, the part, and many other factors affecting his work.

The film fashion of make-up affected theatre make-up very strongly. Considering the experience of the past years and the present knowledge of the influence of lighting upon make-up together with the specific properties of film negatives, it may be said that there need not be any considerable difference between theatre and film make-up.

In the early years of television a similar situation arose as at the beginning of film. The make-up artists then thought—and the originally used camera tubes exhibiting strange and unexpected reaction to colour, confirmed their ideas—that television requires not only a quite different way of make-up but also entirely different types of make-up. Naturally, the manufacturers of cosmetics did not try to discourage this attitude and developed special kinds of television make-up different from their regular products. Actually any kind of make-up may be used in television with as good results as are achieved in film and theatre, providing the right shade is chosen and properly applied.

Excellent results of the make-up artist's work are never due only to the quality of the special make-up used, but mainly to his skill, knowledge, taste and artistic imagination. Each face represents an individual problem which must always be treated as such. The situation is, however, made easier by the fact that the manufacturers of cosmetics produce the main types of make-up, such as fatty foundation (grease paint), emulsion make-up, liquid powder and pancake in identical colours so that they can be easily blended on the face or on different parts of the body.

This chapter presents basic information about various types of make-up, their characteristics and most suitable means of application, as well as a survey of the make-up artist's implements.

105

8.1. FATTY FOUNDATION

The fatty foundation is a mixture of natural and synthetic oils and waxes, higher aliphatic alcohols, emulsifiers, fillers, pigments and sometimes other special ingredients are also added. It must have good smearing and covering ability. It is used as a foundation make-up for the entire face in colour as well as in monochromatic films, and as a foundation make-up in theatre and television. It is a good base for character make-up when shadows and highlights have to be applied. Fatty foundation together with pancake is the only make-up that blends well with the special plastic mask make-up used for the foam latex casts. It should therefore be applied in such cases where a foam latex cast is used for changing the shape of a facial part and the fine edges of the latex piece blend with the normal skin. The fatty foundation is applied in dabs all over the face and is rubbed on the skin with the fingers or a slightly moist sponge. The applied layer should always be even and very thin. It is advisable to pat the made-up parts lightly with moistened finger-tips.

Fatty foundation is produced in a wide choice of colours.

8.2. EMULSION MAKE-UP

Emulsion make-up lies between fatty foundation and liquid powder. The fatty component is a mixture of natural and synthetic waxes, and oils and is emulsified in water together with the higher aliphatic alcohols. Fillers and pigments are added. The ratio of fat to water is well balanced and maintained by a suitable emulsifier. The character of the emulsion make-up is very similar to that of pancake. Both kinds are very suitable for day make-up, as they can be applied very easily and the final, even colour effect is excellent. Emulsion make-up may be used either alone or in combination with powder, according to the skin-type. It has weaker covering ability than fatty foundation but can be applied perfectly, leaving the skin very fresh and its texture practically unchanged. This type of make-up is most suitable for the make-up of young faces, children, sportsmen, rustic or working characters. Fixing with powder is sometimes necessary for aristocratic types. Work with emulsion make-up is very quick and it is advisable to use it as a foundation make-up for the chorus. It may also be applied on the powdered fatty foundation to give the face a fresher look. The made-up part is evenly coloured without any spots and blemishes. Emulsion make-up is especially suitable for making up large body areas. The skin retains its life-like look and the make-up is re-sistant to water. Emulsion make-up is applied with a fine sponge and is then evenly distributed with a dry, clean hand. Soiling of costumes is prevented by removing the surplus with a piece of soft flannel after it has dried completely.

8.3. LIQUID POWDER

Liquid powder contains only water-soluble components, ethyl alcohol and other polyalcohols, such as glycerol, and finely dispersed fillers and pigments. These components settle on standing so the mixture must be shaken well before use to avoid colour distortion of the various portions of the product. Liquid powder has excellent covering power, keeps well on the skin and maintains its natural matt texture. It is used for rapid make-up of the exposed parts of the body such as the throat, shoulders, arms and legs. It may also be used in combination with fatty foundation or it may even replace it. Liquid powder is also suitable for making up men in the chorus, and as a foundation make-up of peasant men and women. It blends well with transparent make-up and is miscible with it in all proportions.

The way of application is the same as with emulsion make-up — a sponge is best.

8.4. PANCAKE

Pancake is a solid emulsion with properties similar to emulsion make-up. It also contains fatty and water-soluble components together with fillers, binding agents and pigments. An emulsifier is also present to emulsify the fatty components with those that are insoluble in water when pancake is moistened. Its covering power is almost the same as that of the fatty foundation but the texture of the skin is enhanced much more and its life-like look is retained. Adhesion to the skin is perfect and it spreads very well. It is usually applied with a moist sponge and before it is completely dry it is brushed with a powder brush or wiped with a piece of soft flannel to achieve an even, smooth surface.

It is used instead of fatty foundation as its application is much easier and quicker. For corrective make-up all shadows and highlights may be applied on a clean, dry face, free of any make-up and then apply pancake over the entire face. The shadows and highlights are barely visible and the final effect is perfectly natural as all colours blend with pancake. It is most suitable to use it for the make-up of large areas or for the entire body. The final result is excellent, even in the very dark shades which are very troublesome with other make-up.

The thickness of the layer depends on the amount of water used for dilution of pancake before its application with a moist sponge; very subtle or heavier layers may be achieved.

Pancake is resistant to water and is therefore used for filming in rain or for swimming scenes, etc. It may also be used as a day make-up.

8.5. TRANSPARENT MAKE-UP

Transparent make-up contains only water-soluble components. It is produced in many shades and is usually used for skin retaining its natural texture and pigmentation. It is comparatively resistant to water and is used for shots when the actor comes into contact with water. It is often used for sun-tanning of peasant men and women or for older characters. It is applied with a sponge, and is hard to remove, especially the darker shades, as it colours the skin.

8.6. FLUID FATTY MAKE-UP

This make-up contains only fatty components, fillers and pigments which also settle and it must also be shaken before use. It is absolutely waterproof and is used almost exclusively for filming scenes in water. The skin acquires a very oily look, so that this type of make-up is also used to characterize certain types of working conditions. It is very rarely used nowadays because it has been replaced by emulsion make-up or by pancake.

8.7. PLASTIC MASK FOUNDATION MAKE-UP

This type of make-up is used only for making-up foam latex casts. The shade must correspond to that of the foundation make-up of the remaining parts of the face. It is usually combined with fatty foundation and must therefore be miscible with it in all proportions. It must not change its colour when applied to the latex piece.

Normal fatty foundation acquires a greyish hue when in contact with foam latex. It is applied with a dry sponge. Recently it has been replaced by the pancake type of make-up.

8.8. COMPRESSED POWDER

Compressed powders contain insoluble silicates, for example talc and kaolin, non-toxic stearates and pigments. They spread well, their adhesion to the skin is perfect, they blend colours and give the skin a natural matt shine. They are applied to the skin on previously applied cream or foundation make-up, which can be replaced by them in some cases. They make a very subtle, almost imperceptible layer. Compressed powder is applied with a brush or a flat powder puff. Compressed powders are much favoured in recent years. They are used for quick make-up of the parts around the mouth and eyes, and the exposed parts of the body, such as the throat, shoulders, arms and legs of ballet dancers. They are also used for shadowing of eyelids, not only in film, theatre and television, but also for day make-up. They are available in many shades of skin tints, and in a number of auxiliary colours such as brown, grey, blue, green, grey-blue, azure, etc.

8.9. POWDER

Powders are used to fix the made-up parts and to diminish shine. They should always be a shade lighter than the make-up and should be translucent. They must never be used for changing the colour of the foundation, and must never be applied by rubbing or on damp foundation, as they would form blotches which would be difficult to remove. A velour powder puff is best for application of powders..

Talc is used sometimes for the make-up of older types, as it gives the skin a whitish, translucent tint. It is also used to add a matt shine to the foam latex pieces. Bald heads made of foam latex, suede or other material are powdered with talc, and brushed.

8.10. COVERING CREAMS

Covering creams are more solid and have much greater covering power than other types of make-up. They are produced in skin colour shades, usually in yellowish, peachy, pinkish or light brown tones and are used to conceal minor blemishes of the skin, such as blackheads, pimples, warts, lines, scars, dark marks and blue rings under the eyes. They are applied with a brush on smaller areas and with the fingers on larger ones. They are also used as highlights to achieve an impression of a thin face. The colours of covering creams must always correspond to those of the skin and not to the colour of the foundation make-up used.

8.11. ADHESIVE PASTES

Adhesive pastes are mixtures of natural waxes and esters of poly-alcohols, of solid consistence and suitable melting-point. They are used to achieve rapid minor shape changes of parts of the face or body (deformations of the nose, forehead, cheeks, the eyes, ageing, etc.). They have excellent adhesion to the skin and are not melted by body temperature or by the temperature of the environment. Tears, rain and cold water have no effect upon them. They are pliable and elastic and do not obstruct any movement of the facial muscles. They are applied with the fingers

109

or a spatula. They hold fast even on the most sensitive parts of the face, the eyelids, where other accessories cannot be fixed satisfactorily. They are miscible with the foundation make-up and can therefore acquire the same tint as the other parts of the face. However, they can be damaged very easily by a careless touch. Adhesive paste may be used instead of spirit gum for fixing a short cut beard, which looks quite natural when fixed by this technique. It can be removed from the face with a wad of cotton wool.

8.12. AUXILIARY MAKE-UP

Auxiliary make-up completes and helps to create a character foundation make-up. It is produced in a large number of shades, except in skin tones, and the most important are all shades of red, brown, grey, blue and green. It is usually applied on the foundation make-up. When pancake is used, however, it is applied directly on the skin, prior to pancake application.

Brown and *red–brown shades* are used for shadowing too broad or prominent parts or for tracing lines and hollows. They are applied with a flat brush and patted or rubbed with the fingers.

Grey and *grey–brown shades* are used to make shadows in the eyeholes of the older characters and for creating an impression of deeper hollows and ridges. Grey tone is used to enhance the beard area of older characters. They are applied with a brush or with the fingers.

Blue, *grey–blue*, *golden* and *silver* shadows are used to enhance the upper lids of women, the veins and rings under the eyes. In colour film and in the theatre they may also be used to stress the beard area in the faces of young and middle-aged men. Application is the same as in the case of grey tones.

Cream rouges. Light and brilliant shades of red are applied on the cheeks and lips. Bluish or violet shades of red are used only for the lips of older women. Pastel shades are used for the make-up of young girls and children. Pastel red–brown shades are used to enhance the colour of lips of ordinary men and women. The impression of a fat face can also be achieved by the clever application of red on the cheeks.

Dry rouge is applied on the powdered parts made up by the foundation make-up in colour film and on the stage. It is sometimes used for day make-up to emphasize the shape of the cheek bones.

Both cream as well as dry rouge should always correspond in colour to the colour of the lipstick.

Terracotta red is rusty brown with a faint violet hue and is used on the cheeks and nose of older characters to achieve the impression of a network of tiny broken blood vessels and a veiny complexion. When applied on the eyelids an impression of a drunkard's or diseased eyes is achieved. This shade of red mixed with auxiliary rusty brown make-up yields the right shade for making up healthy rustic types. It is applied with a dry sponge or by patting with the finger tips.

8.13. EYEBROW AND LIP PENCILS

Eyebrows, eyes, hairlines and fine beards are drawn with black, brown or grey make-up pencils or lines. Their colour should always correspond to the colour of the hair and eyebrows. To trace fine lines and wrinkles, brown or red–brown pencils should be used. Black lines look unnatural and exaggerated. A red pencil is used to outline the shape of lips or of a wound.

The length and sharpness of the tip of the pencil changes with the type of the line traced.

8.14. MASCARA

Mascara is made in various forms, for example in solid cakes that are applied with a moist brush, cream or aqueous liquid types that are available together with a plastic spiral, mascara brush, either normal or spiral-shaped.

Some manufacturers produce mascara containing very fine, short natural or synthetic filaments which are applied to the eyelashes with a spiral brush. The fine filaments hold on the lashes and lengthen them several millimetres.

Mascara is produced in various shades, most frequently black, grey or brown, sometimes even green, blue and violet. They are used to make up the eyelashes and to enhance the hair line for men's make-up.

An impression of an unshaven face may be achieved by spraying aqueous liquid mascara on the beard area.

8.15. EYE-SHADOWS

Eye-shadows are used to enlarge small eyes, to enhance sunken eyes or to correct eyelids which are too heavy. They are manufactured in many shades, either in a liquid or in a solid form. Shades are changing with contemporary fashion.

8.16. EYE-LINERS

The upper and lower lids are lined very near the eyelashes. The most suitable eye-liners come in the shape of pencils. They are also made in liquid form. They may be obtained in various colours which should always correspond to the colour of the lashes or the eye shadows.

8.17. LIPSTICKS

Lipstick used for film, theatre and television need not be so kiss-proof as the ones used for day make-up. They should, however, be greasy enough so as not to dry the lips. Lipsticks should always give the lips a fine, fresh appearance, important for close-up. They are produced in many colours from which the make-up man must choose the most suitable ones, chiefly regarding the type of the artiste's role, the kind of lighting, and the negatives used. These, as well as the common criteria for the quality of lipsticks, must always be meticulously respected.

8.18. NAIL LACQUERS

Make-up should be completed with well-shaped and polished finger-nails. Nail lacquers are manufactured in many shades, transparent as well as pigmented ones having a pearly lustre.

The colour of nail-polish should always harmonize with the lipstick colour. Well-manicured hands are an important feature in complete make-up. Ugly-shaped or damaged fingernails can be concealed by artificial ones.

8.19. HAIR LACQUERS

Hair lacquers are a very important aid for shaping the hair-do of men and women. Hair made of live as well as of dead hair may be modelled better, and the hair is more lustrous. The lacquers make an invisible net on the hair, which prevents the hair-do from damage. The lacquers should always be finely atomized so as not to form little droplets on the hair and make it sticky.

Hair lacquers are available in aerosols which disperse the lacquer in the form of very fine mist. The lacquers can be either colourless, coloured or can contain particles of metal powders.

8.20. THE MAKE-UP ARTIST'S IMPLEMENTS

The following list comprises the basic aids of any make-up artist's equipment.

8.20.1. *Make-up*
  Foundation make-up
   Fatty foundation in jars
   Fatty foundation in the form of panstik
   Emulsion make-up

112

Pancake
Transparent make-up
Liquid powder
Liquid fatty foundation
Powder puffs — flat, made of plush or velour; for application of
  powder by patting.

Auxiliary and character make-up
  Covering creams
  Plastic pastes — used to achieve minor plastic changes in the soft
    parts of the face such as lines and wrinkles around the eyes,
    pouches under the eyes, etc.
Collodion — a highly volatile solution of nitrocellulose; it is used
    mainly to imitate wrinkled skin and scars. It is sometimes used in
    combination with fine cotton fabric, tulle or çotton wool.
  Nose putty — used to obtain plastic changes of the nose, forehead,
    chin, etc.
  Tooth enamel — chiefly white or yellowish for covering dental flaws,
    or brown and black to achieve the impression of a toothless
    mouth.
  Artificial blood
  Fish air vesicle — for imitation of scars.
  Foam latex accessories
  Pencil liners
  Hair whitener either in the form of a lacquer or brilliantine. It is used
    to whiten or grey the hair for old-age make-up.
  Talcum powder
  Plastic mask make-up
  Metal powders for achieving hair lustre are available in various
    colours — mainly silver or golden, but also green, blue, dark red
    or copper.
  Mineral oil for preparing plastic mask make-up used for the make-up
    of foam latex pieces and for imitating perspiration, instead of
    the formerly used glycerine.
Gelatine capsules for achieving the effect of bleeding from the mouth.

Make-up of the eyes
  Mascara
  Eyeshadows
  Eye-liners
  False eyelashes in various sizes and colours of different length and
    thickness of the lashes. They are mainly brown and black, rarely
    blue, green or violet.

113

Liquid adhesive for applying false eyelashes.

Small scissors

Foreceps — pointed for epilation of the eyebrows, flat for fixing foam latex pieces.

Eyelash curler — the rubber lining of the rims must be perfect to prevent breaking of the lashes.

Eyedroppers

Rouges

Lipsticks — light, medium, dark, extra dark.

Cheek rouges

Lipstick containers

Lipstick wands

8.20.2. *Brushes*

Brushes of various shapes and sizes, round and flat, usually made of marten, squirrel, camel or Chinese hair:

Lipbrushes

Make-up shading brushes

Spirit gum brushes

Mascara brushes

Powder brushes

Hairbrushes

Toothbrushes

Nailbrushes

8.20.3. *Hair Materials*

Crêpe hair of various colours, straight and kinked, made of hairs or vegetable fibre for beards, and other types of hairpieces, for blending finished beards, whiskers and moustaches.

Crêpe hair — light grey, medium grey, dark grey, medium brown, white.

Combs of various shapes and lengths, pointed, thin and thick.

Hairpins

Forceps

Brilliantine

Witch hazel

Atomizers

Hair nets

Bandage

Curling irons: round, with a metal handle for curling hair; flat and pointed, for hair dressing.

Curl stick — a conical wooden stick for making hair curls.
Hair lacquers — coloured, colourless.
Barber shears
Rubber bands for hair dressing.
Curlers

8.20.4. *Adhesives*

Spirit gum is a solution of mastic resin in ether. It is used for fixing wigs and other hairpieces; it is very stable, resistant to perspiration and water, dries quickly and has excellent adhesive power. It is sometimes too glossy and must always be made up properly.

Spirit lacquer for fixing hairpieces. Sometimes used in combination with spirit gum to control drying.

Rubber adhesive — used for fixing foam latex pieces, especially on parts which are strained mechanically. The volatile solutions of adhesive should always be kept in bottles with ground stoppers with fixed brushes.

8.20.5. *Solvents and Other Liquids*

Acetone — as a cleanser for wigs and foam latex pieces.

Alcohol — containing a disinfectant for skin disinfection.

Petroleum ether as a degreasing agent or for removing traces of adhesives after the use of foam latex accessories.

Ether for diluting mastic solutions.

Glycerol or its mixture with water, for making false tears and perspiration. It it applied with a sponge or an eyedropper. A mixture of glycerol with water of suitable viscosity and colour may be used as artificial blood for gunshot — and other bleeding — wounds.

Hydrogen peroxide for bleaching hair, eyebrows, etc.

Boric acid (aqueous solution) for washing mascara out of the eye.

8.20.6. *Make-up Removers*
Cleansing lotion
Cold cream
Disinfectant cleansing lotion
Vaseline

8.20.7. *Nail Polishing*
Nailpolishes — transparent, pigmented, with a pearly lustre.
Nailpolish remover
Nourishing cream
Nail file.

8.20.8. *Other Aids*
Spatulas
Jars for brushes
Tape measure
Magnifying mirror for make-up of eyes.
Capes, towels and wraps protecting the actor's costume from soiling
with make-up, powder etc.
Wig stand for *wigs*.
Swivelling and collapsible stand with wooden blocks for wig and
hair-piece making.
Trays for crêpe, make-up, brushes.

8.20.9. *Miscellaneous*
Fabric
Muslin silk or nylon or French tulle for skin fixation and uplifting of
limp parts of the face, especially of the cheeks.
Gauze for wigmaking, may be replaced with cambric muslin.
Cotton wool — in combination with adhesives may be used to achieve
various plastic effects; it is also used for cleansing the skin.
Cellulose wadding tufts pointed at both ends are used instead of
lining pencils; they are dipped in paint or auxiliary make-up and
used chiefly for applying eyeshadows.
Soap
Razor blades
Shaving creams
Toupee band double-faced adhesive used for attaching mous-
taches, sideburns and whiskers, mainly in comedy shows.
Pins — safety as well as straight ones.
Needles
Thread
Bobbypins
Gummed labels

9. FOAM LATEX ACCESSORIES

THE ever-increasing artistic and technical demands of film, television and theatre, are introducing new methods into all aspects.

One of the results of this process is the development of a new technology for making foam rubber accessories for make-up, which considerably extend the make-up artist's possibilities. With the help of foam latex accessories some effects may be achieved, which prior to the discovery of this particular rubber were practically unattainable, e.g. in the process of ageing the make-up artist can entirely change the shape of certain parts of the actor's face and thus achieve a faithful impression of gradual ageing. Grotesque masks can be obtained with the help of foam latex pieces and sometimes the realization of the dramatist's idea depends on the use of such material.

Foam latex products became an indispensable aid within the last few years for the solution of many problems of make-up.

All other accessories used so far for achieving changes of shape of the actor's face, or its parts, hindered the movement of the facial muscles and gave a torpid, unnatural appearance to the face. They could not be used for faithful portrayals of authentic characters.

The latex foam pieces are porous, soft and elastic, and they do not hamper the natural movement of the facial muscles. They may be used in black and white as well as in colour films, in television and on the stage. They can be tinted to any required shade and easily made up. Fixing on the actor's face is not difficult and the fine edges of latex pieces blend imperceptibly with the skin.

To-date latex pieces are the ideal make-up accessories which resemble all aspects of the skin most closely.

It would be wrong, however, to overestimate their possibilities. They should be used only in cases in which a real change of character is to be achieved and/or an authentic person has to be accurately portrayed, or when it is easier to use the latex piece, rather then to try to achieve the required effect by classical means. Sometimes, however, the unnecessary use of a latex piece may bring a lot of undesired complications. This must always be kept in mind and the make-up artist has to estimate carefully the proper use of foam latex in appropriate situations.

This chapter contains the basic information about the procedures, technique and means of application of the foam latex accessories and is intended to help the reader in this new and relatively difficult branch of make-up technique.

9.1. RUBBER

The raw material for the production of latex accessories for make-up is rubber. It is a high polymer found in the gum of rubber trees. Many kinds of tropical plants contain a similar substance, but only *Hevea brasiliensis*, the *Indian rubber tree*, is worth exploiting.

For the manufacture of foam latex products only latex dispersion is used. It is a white, cream-like emulsion with a strong ammoniacal odour.

9.2. PREPARATION OF FOAM LATEX ACCESSORIES

The technique has the following phases:
1. Taking a cast of the actor's face or of the required part of the face.
2. Preparation of the plaster mould and its finishing for modelling.
3. Modelling of the required changes on the cast.
4. Preparation of the mould for the latex cast.
5. Preparation of the foam latex cast.
6. Fixing the cast on the face.
7. Make-up of the cast.

9.2.1. *Casts of the Actor's Face*

The actor, who is to represent a certain character, the faithful portrayal of whom requires changes in the shape of the actor's face, must have a plaster cast of his face taken. The cavity obtained is used as a mould for making the core. The cavity is allowed to set, shellac is applied to its inner surface and it is filled with plaster. After the plaster mixture sets, the cavity is carefully broken. Care must be taken not to damage the core. The required change of the actor's features are then modelled on the core. It is advisable to fix the core into the upper part of a metal frame, before any alterations are started on it. After the alterations have been finished, the bottom part of the metal frame is fixed on the upper part (the core with the alterations) and the metal frame is filled with plaster. When the plaster sets, both parts of the metal frame are separated and the alteration is removed. In the plaster mould there is a cavity corresponding with the alteration. This cavity is filled with foam latex, the mould is shut and is allowed to cure. When curing is finished, a latex cast is obtained and it can be fixed on the actor's face whenever necessary.

9.2.1.1. *Procedure of casting.* Several rules of correct casting must be observed to achieve a flawless cast, which is the most important factor affecting the final shape of the foam latex piece.

The actor who is going to have the cast of his face taken must be completely relaxed. It is best to sit in a comfortable, semi-reclining position, some time before the actual casting is started. The head must be propped up in such a position that there is no danger that the completed cast, which is often quite heavy, will mis-shape the soft parts of the face. The actor should breathe slowly and evenly during casting and should keep his face very still.

A thin layer of petroleum jelly has to be applied to the face (or on the particular part which is to be cast), especially round the eyes, on the eyebrows, lashes and hair. As a rule, two or more layers of plaster must be used to make a reliable cast. For the first layer, the plaster mixture must be very thin and free from bubbles, for it has to copy faithfully all the lines, furrows and other details of the actor's complexion. For the subsequent layers the plaster mixture may be thicker. It is advisable to apply the plaster mixture with a brush on the parts around the nostrils, taking care to keep them free for breathing. No glass or other tubes must be inserted into the nose, because they enlarge the nostrils and the final latex piece would not be exact, and its fixing to the face would then be very difficult (Figs. 78–80).

If the plaster mixture has been correctly prepared, the cast may be taken off the face within 10 or 15 minutes, the right moment being when

FIGS. 78–80. TAKING CASTS OF THE ACTOR'S FACE

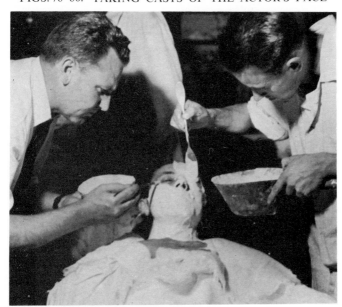

FIG. 78. The application of the first plaster layer.

119

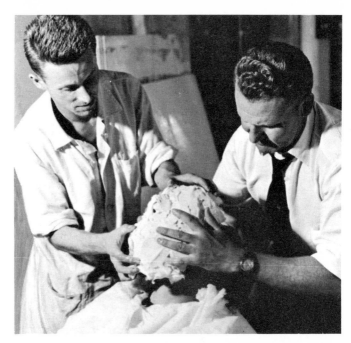

FIG. 79. The cast before removing it from the face.

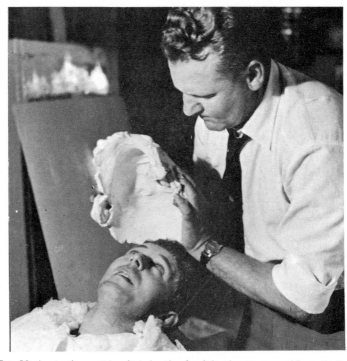

FIG. 80. A negative cast (cavity) shortly after it has been removed from the face.

120

the plaster starts to get warm. If the cast is left on the face too long, it shrinks a little, removal is more difficult, and the cast may easily be damaged. The cast should be carefully loosened first on the chin, and then bit by bit upwards towards the forehead.

9.2.2. *Preparation of the Plaster Mould and its Finishing for Modelling*

For a clearer illustration the preparation of a plaster mould for an alteration to the forehead will be described. The positive plaster cast of the forehead is placed in the lower part of the metal frame; care must be taken to maintain its back obliquely. The plaster cast is placed on a layer of modelling clay, and all empty spots of the frame are also filled with

FIG. 81. The preparation of a positive model from a negative cast.

clay. Shellac is then applied on the cast of the forehead and a mould of two or more pieces is prepared in the following way: the forehead is divided in two or three parts with a cylinder of modelling clay (about 1 cm in diameter). A lubricant is then applied on the forehead and plaster is poured in. The metal guide rods, on which the upper part of the frame slides into position, are placed in the lower part of the metal frame.

The pieces of a plaster mould obtained are then fixed in the upper part of a metal casting frame, shellac is applied to them and plaster is poured in. After it has set properly, the frame is opened and a core of the forehead is obtained (Fig. 81). It is left in the upper part of the metal frame and the required changes are modelled on it. To the rest of the cast (without the alteration) a lubricant is applied with a brush. The upper part is

FIG. 82. Positive plaster model of the actor's face.

then fitted to the negative part of the metal casting frame, which is filled with plaster. The frame is opened after the plaster has set (usually 20 minutes) and the alteration is removed. The latex mixture is then poured into the plaster mould obtained, which has been allowed to dry thoroughly.

Drying of the mould takes several days and it is best to let it dry at room temperature. Higher temperatures may cause deformations of the moulds and the resulting latex cast is not exact, because the negative and positive parts of the moulds do not fit together properly. High temperature may even cause chemical changes of the plaster and thus decrease the durability of the mould.

If the mould is deformed, the whole process must be repeated to obtain an accurate one. The preparation of moulds is not cheap and it is time-consuming. All factors diminishing the durability of moulds should therefore be avoided (Fig. 82).

9.2.3. *Modelling*

Modelling facial changes is a very subtle process and it should always be kept in mind that only changes which are absolutely necessary should be made. It may happen that the newly modelled part of the face may sometimes appear exaggerated compared with the rest of the face. Therefore in each case, when an alteration is required, it must fully harmonize with the other features and it should never be attempted without basic knowledge of the facial anatomy.

The alteration is effected by a technique similar to that by which a sculptor creates a portrait. The approach and the final aims are, however, different. The sculptor portrays the face maintaining its harmony among the individual parts and features. He enlivens the dead matter by impressing tension or tranquillity into the portrait, according to his imagination and his artistic aim. The sculpture represents his ideas and conceptions and the portrait remains unchanged for ever.

The base of the latex piece, however, is the actor's face. It is the actor who enlivens the latex piece with the movements of his facial muscles and with his acting. The actor can—in a sense—complete the final effect of the rubber mask, or can completely alter its appearance. It is therefore necessary to bear in mind all the factors affecting the final result while the mask is being prepared and fixed on the face.

The most important of these factors are the shape and location of the facial muscles and their movement, and the possibility to control the mask by the movements of the respective muscles.

A complete latex mask, covering the entire face, is seldom made. As a rule the individual parts of the face are changed more often. If the required foam latex piece is more complicated, the alteration is carried out on the plaster cast of the entire face or of the head. This helps to decide which parts will be modelled, how they will be joined together and how the complete mask will be fixed on the face with regard to the facial muscles. The alteration on the cast of the entire face is also a good guide for making the necessary hairpieces and wigs.

Plasticine is a very good modelling material, because it is very soft, elastic and dries slowly. The surface of the modelled parts may be corrected and finished much better than with modelling clay. Sometimes, however, modelling clay is preferred, especially when thicker layers or vertical alterations are required.

9.2.3.1. *Modelling clay.* Modelling clay should always be quite smooth, elastic, soft and free from hard lumps. It must be kept moist, otherwise it would crack, and must be kept wet while modelling. The model must be kept moist until it is set in the mould and plaster poured over it, otherwise it will crack. When work is stopped, the clay must be sprayed with water and wrapped in wet cloth or in plastic sheets. It should be kept in a wooden box with a metal lid. Dry modelling clay is too hard and it is difficult to render it usable again by kneading with water. Well-kneaded, moist clay is a very good modelling material; it is harder than plasticine, so that even thick vertical layers maintain their shape.

9.2.3.2. *Plasticine.* Plasticine can be prepared as follows: 8 parts by weight of beeswax are mixed with 1 part by weight of lard. The mixture is warmed, stirred slowly and constantly until uniformly melted, and talc is slowly added. The cooled mixture is soft and pliable.

9.2.3.3. *General advice.* The modelled part should keep the facial muscles as free as possible and should never run transversly across them. The latex piece should never commence in the centre of a large flat area, such as the forehead or the cheek. Even if its edges are very fine and imperceptible it is impossible to achieve absolutely identical movements of the live muscle with the latex piece.

It is most important to model the edges of the piece very thinly, so that the latex cast can be blended quite imperceptibly with the skin in its vicinity. Meticulous care in this phase of the work saves a lot of trouble when the moulds and the latex pieces are made. The structure and porosity of the skin should be carefully imitated on the latex piece. Rubber sponges of different grain are used to achieve the impression of pores and they are slightly pressed on the surface of the finished model, thus making tiny dents in the soft material.

When plasticine is used for the modelled part it should be applied with a sculptor's spatula or with wire loops of required shape and size. The surface is usually smoothed with slightly moist or greasy fingers.

There is, however, no guide for the model as such. It depends solely on the dexterity, skill, artistic imagination, sense of proportion and anatomical knowledge of the make-up artist.

9.2.4. *Preparation of the Plaster Moulds for the Latex Cast*

The technology of foam latex is closely connected with suitable moulds. The mould material affects the quality and properties of the final foam latex product to a considerable extent. The most suitable moulds for this technique are made of plaster. They have a number of advantages. Plaster is very cheap and easily available, and the moulds can be made very precisely and rapidly.

While mixing plaster with water, the two components react immediately, and the mixture gets warm during the reaction. Its volume increases slightly (by 1 per cent) and after a while it sets. This process differs from modelling clay, which sets by drying.

9.2.4.1. *Mixing plaster with water.* Powdered plaster is always poured slowly in a thin, continuous stream into water as long as the small heaps of plaster that are formed on the surface of water accept it. The mixture must be properly stirred to obtain a smooth, thick, and soft paste. It is best to let it stand for a short while before use. Water must never be poured into plaster, because lumps would form, which are very difficult to break. Dry plaster of good quality needs more water for mixing than moist plaster. The temperature of the soft or hard water should be about 10–25°C. Acid water, or water containing more sulphate ions, speeds the reaction.

9.2.4.2. *Control of the setting time.* It is possible to control the setting time of plaster. As a rule slower setting is more desirable, because more time can be gained to accomplish all necessary arrangements connected with the making of moulds. Setting may be delayed by addition of very thin liquid glue. This is the most reliable and convenient method.

Thin glue is prepared by soaking 500 g of blue in 3 l. of cold water for 24 hours. Then 150 g of slaked lime are added, the mixture is warmed and boiled a little. This is very important, as otherwise the mixture would gelatinize after cooling. Correctly prepared thin glue must be liquid. It is added to the water used for mixing plaster. The ratio must, however, be found empirically. The test is carried out in the following way: 50–100 ml thin glue are added to 1 l. water, the required amount of plaster mixture is prepared, and the setting time is noted. According to the result of this test, the amount of thin glue may be increased, if setting has been too rapid, or less glue may be used if setting has been too slow. Certain limits must not be exceeded, however, because the plaster mixture would either remain soft, or setting would be so slow that a certain amount of water would evaporate and cracks would subsequently appear in the moulds. Any blemishes that appear in the moulds must be very carefully removed; this is often very tiresome. Plaster sets more slowly when molasses or borax are added; kitchen salt or alum accelerate setting time.

9.2.4.3. *Increase of the solidity and elasticity of plaster.* Set plaster is very fragile and can easily be damaged. The resistance and endurance of the moulds may be increased by adding 5–10 per cent of an aqueous dispersion of polyvinyl acetate to the water used for mixing plaster. The polyvinyl acetate dispersion fills the pores of the mould, the set products achieve a certain elasticity and their surface is absolutely smooth.

9.2.4.4. *Retouching of the moulds.* The plaster moulds almost always have some minor superficial blemishes, such as blisters and dimples, caused by air bubbles enclosed in the plaster, or "seams" and other flaws, which must be carefully retouched leaving no traces of interference in the finished moulds. It is most important not to touch the surface of the mould in the vicinity of the corrected blemish. Brushes, small chisels and scrapers, emery paper, etc., are used for retouching.

Two-piece moulds are normally used for casting of foam latex accessories. The cavity is filled with the latex mixture and the core is used as an upper cover. The moulds should always be made in such a manner that the latex casts may easily be removed therefrom. In some cases it is advisable to fix the core into a metal frame to maintain the most suitable angle. It is very convenient to use the frames for bigger casts, because the guiding rods of the frame permit accurate fixing of both parts.

9.2.4.5. *How to store plaster.* Plaster must be stored in a dry place, because it is very hygroscopic (absorbs water very readily) and atmospheric moisture is sufficient to form small lumps of set plaster in containers which are stored in a damp place. The lumps are very difficult to break and the quality of plaster deteriorates. Moist plaster sets very rapidly after mixing with water and it is hardly usable.

9.2.4.6. *Release agents.* Before the mould is filled with the latex mixture, it must be treated with a release agent, which prevents the mixture from sticking to the walls of the moulds.

A large number of materials may be used as release agents. A 2 per cent solution of beeswax, or carnauba or mineral wax dissolved in petrol or trichlorethylene is used most frequently. If aqueous release agents are preferred, a 5 per cent solution of polyvinyl alcohol together with a metal stearate solution (such as zinc stearate) may be used. Instead of polyvinyl alcohol it is also possible to use carboxymethylcellulose.

The following mixture of polyvinyl alcohol and soap is also a very good release agent: 1 or 1·5 parts by weight of polyvinyl alcohol are dissolved and boiled in 10 parts by weight of water. 0·1–0·2 parts by weight of pulverized or chipped coconut soap are added, the mixture is cooled to 60–70°C, and 10 parts by weight of ethyl alcohol are poured in with constant stirring. This release agent dries very quickly, and separates very well.

If none of the above-mentioned agents is available, colourless floor- or shoe-polish may be used. A soap solution or a thin soap paste, prepared as follows, also yields good results. 50–100 g of soap chips are boiled in 500 ml water while stirring. A thin soap paste is obtained which serves well as a release agent.

Stearine dissolved in kerosene may also be used. Preparation is very simple: 10 parts by weight of stearine are heated; when it softens, 3 parts by weight of kerosene are added and the mixture is stirred. This release agent is highly flammable, so it might be advisable to use an alternative: 35 parts by weight turpentine are warmed, 12 parts by weight of wax paraffin, together with 6 parts by weight of ceresine and 10 parts by weight of carnauba wax are finely grated and added to the warm turpentine. The mixture is heated until all chips are melted and stirring is continued until cool.

9.2.5. *Preparation of the Latex Cast*

The foam latex casts are made from natural latex or from a mixture of natural and synthetic latex. The latter should be used particularly for bigger casts of the soft parts of the face and throat.

Depending on the ultimate properties of the latex cast, various ingredients are added. Textile wetting agents are usually used as the expanding agents for foam latex pieces. The wetting agents are the neutral salts of higher aliphatic alcohols or of aliphatic sulphoacids. As a rule a mixture of ultra-accelerators is used, because their mutual activity is more effective than a corresponding amount of only one type of ultra-accelerator.

If powder ingredients are used, they must first be mixed with a wetting agent, carefully rubbed and mixed well. Then latex is poured in and the mixture is well stirred in the electric mixer. It is best to use mixers with controllable speeds. As a rule, $\frac{1}{2}$l. latex mixture at a time can be mixed in a 2 l. bowl.

A high speed should be used at the beginning of mixing and should be decreased to one-quarter towards the end of mixing. The mixture is thus homogenized and no big air bubbles are enclosed. Their presence in the finished cast deteriorates its quality. The speed, however, decreases in any case towards the end of mixing, as the mixture increases in volume and the density and resistance of the foam is greater.

The properties of the latex pieces are affected by the kind and amount of ingredients used, especially by the ultra-accelerators and the expanding agents. Generally, the cast is expanded more when it is mixed more. The expanded volume should not be greater than five times the original volume. The air bubbles should be of the smallest possible size.

The mixing time depends on the amount of the mixture, its composition, the shape and size of the mixer bowl, the shape of the whisk, the number of rotations and on the amount of the wetting agent and its kind. It ranges from 5 to 20 minutes.

When thicker casts are required, it is advisable to add 5–10 ml of a saturated aqueous solution of sodium fluorosilicate per 500 g of latex. This agent prevents collapse of the foam. It should be added approximately 1 minute before the mixing is stopped.

Sulphur	5 g
Zinc oxide	6 g
Ultra-accelerator ZDC	3 g
Ultra-accelerator P extra N	5 g
10% solution of wetting agent	10–20 ml
Latex	500 g

Sometimes it is advisable to use a mixture of natural and synthetic latex. The ratio ranges from 80 per cent of natural and 20 per cent of synthetic latex, to 50 per cent of the natural and 50 per cent of the synthetic. The accessories made from this mixture are softer, lighter, and the exact degree of expansion is reached more easily. *Pipsar 725* a butadiene–styrene rubber, for example, is very good for making rubber accessories.

Natural latex is always added *to* the synthetic dispersion and *never* vice versa. The technique is rather different from that with natural latex. The composition can be prepared as follows:

Pipsar	150 g
Natural latex – *Qualitex*	150 g
Vulcanizing dispersion	13 g
Dispersion of the wetting agent	11 g
Denax	4·5 g
Zinc oxide	9 g
Sodium fluorosilicate	20 g

Vulcanizing dispersion:

Sulphur	14 g
Ultra-accelerator ZDC (P extra N)	12 g
Water	22 g
Ammonium hydroxide	2 g
Wetting agent	2 g

Dispersion of the wetting agent:

Potassium oleate,	10% solution	20 g
Neocal,	10%	10 g

Zinc oxide dispersion:

Zinc oxide	25 g
Water	21 g
Ammonium hydroxide	2 g
Neocal	2 g

Denax dispersion:

Denax	20 g
Water	20 g
Ammonium hydroxide	2 g
Neocal	2 g

Sodium fluorosilicate dispersion:

Sodium fluorosilicate	10 g
Water	36 g
Bentonite	1 g
Ammonium hydroxide	2 g

Pigment dispersion:

Vulcan pigment	10 g
Water	86 g
Ammonium hydroxide	2 g
Neocal	2 g

The dispersion of the vulcanizing ingredients are mixed with the natural and synthetic latex. The mixture is whipped for a few minutes. The dispersion of the wetting agent is added together with the vulcanizing dispersion. Towards the end of whipping the dispersions of zinc oxide and *Denax* are added, and 30 or 40 seconds before the whipping is stopped sodium fluorosilicate dispersion is poured in the mixture. At the same time the speed of the mixer is decreased to avoid large air bubbles appearing in the mixture.

The foamed mixture is poured into a mould that has previously been heated to 40–60°C. According to the amount of sodium fluorosilicate the mixture gels within 3–5 minutes, vulcanization is completed in the hot-air drying kiln within 1–2 hours; curing may be shortened to 20–30 minutes when steam is used instead of hot air.

The whipped and well-foamed latex mixture is then allowed to stand for a few minutes permitting the enclosed air bubbles to escape. It is then slowly poured into the cavity. Care should be taken not to enclose an "air-cushion" or bubbles in the cast, which decreases its quality, and sometimes a cast with entrapped bubbles cannot be used at all. The mould

129

is then slowly and carefully closed and allowed to cure. The core should evenly squeeze out a little surplus latex mixture along the brim of the mould. If a large amount appears, the core does not fit properly properly into the cavity and the edges of the cast will be too thick. If none or very little surplus is squeezed out, it means that the amount of latex has been insufficient and that not all the cavities of the mould have been filled properly.

9.2.5.1. *Vulcanization.* It is best to cure the foam latex product in a hot-air kiln at temperatures ranging from 80 to 140°C. The curing temperature is one of the most important factors which affect the curing time as well as the quality of the final foam latex cast. Lower curing temperatures (within the temperature range in question) as a rule, prolong vulcanization. Higher temperatures, however, yield harder casts. In addition to the curing temperature, the time of vulcanization depends upon the size of the latex cast, on the amount and type of the ultra-accelerators used and on the other vulcanizing ingredients. The material of the moulds and the thickness of their walls also affect vulcanization.

The best results are obtained when curing takes place in the plaster moulds. They are porous and can therefore absorb a certain amount of the water present in the latex mixture. In addition to that, steam that appears during the curing may diffuse freely through the pores of the mould and does not increase the internal pressure. Worse results were obtained in metal moulds. After the curing has been finished the mould is unscrewed and slowly opened. Completion of vulcanization is tested with a finger-nail. If complete, the deformation instantly returns to its original level and no mark is left on the cast. In any case it is advisable to leave the cast on the core for at least one hour at 40°C for drying. Sometimes curing may be completed by boiling the cast for a while in water.

The vulcanized latex cast is washed in luke-warm water, and allowed to dry at room temperature. However, this is not necessary and the pieces may be applied to the face without washing.

Vulcanization must be carried out with the utmost care. Wrongly cured casts are not elastic and can be deformed even by the slightest touch. Casts cured for too long have low mechanical resistance, can easily be damaged and lose their elasticity very quickly. The average curing time ranges between 3–8 hours.

Water curing, which has been sometimes used, has many disadvantages, so that it has been abandoned. Water lowers the durability of the moulds more than the stream of hot air. The moulds can be protected with a waterproof rubber insulating coat, but it is very disagreeable to handle the heavy hot moulds and take them out of the boiling water-bath. Though the foam latex casts, vulcanized in boiling water, are softer, they shrink much more than the casts vulcanized in hot air.

9.2.6. *Fixing of the Foam Latex Piece*

The excess rubber is carefully cut off the washed and dried latex piece, leaving the thinnest possible edges, so that blending with the skin after its fixing on the face is imperceptible.

The foam latex casts are gummed onto clean skin free from any grease. Before it is fixed, the latex piece is placed onto the particular part of the face which is to be altered, and the outline of the piece is traced on the skin with a make-up liner. Spirit gum is applied on the outlined area with a soft brush. A special adhesive is used only for prolonged fixation of the more complicated masks on large areas of the face and of the throat. The adhesive is applied to the inside of the cast, leaving 3 or 5 mm of the edges dry, because the adhesive damages the thin edges, which then roll up and stick together. Spirit gum does not corrode the casts and the durability of the edges is therefore much greater. It is advisable to use the same spirit gum which is used for fixing wigs and hairpieces, in cases where the cast is not moved by the vivid play of the facial muscles. It can be used for fixing latex pieces on the nose, the chin, etc.

After the cast has been fixed in its place, the edges are carefully lifted with a spatula or with forceps, gum is thinly applied on them and they are gently pressed onto the skin (Figs. 83–90).

Gum need not be applied to the entire inner surface of the cast in every case; it should not be applied to the large casts, because it hampers the respiration of the skin too much. The amount of gum depends on the location and on the shape of the cast and on the movement of the respective facial muscles. However, gum must be applied to the edges of the piece in each case.

9.2.6.1. *Blending of the latex piece with the skin.*
Between the fixed foam latex cast and the skin of the face there may always be observed a faint, sometimes almost imperceptible line where the piece meets the skin, even if the edges of the latex accessory are very thin. This line could be very dangerous in close-ups, betraying the false piece and thus spoiling the make-up man's efforts completely.

Quite imperceptible blending of the edges of the foam latex cast with the skin is therefore neccessary. It can be achieved with the help of a covering paste.

The covering paste is a mixture of *Revertex* and very finely pulverized kaolin, tinted to a suitable colour, usually a shade lighter than foundation make-up. It is filled in tubes. It is advisable to keep it in a cool, dark place or immersed in cold water, as it is perishable at room temperature, especially in the summer.

Before use, a dab of the paste is squeezed into a clean porcelain dish where it is left for a moment to achieve suitable viscosity. The paste is

FIGS. 83–90. THE PROCEDURE OF
MAKING A MASK WITH THE
HELP OF FOAM LATEX PIECES

FIG. 83. The actor's natural appearance.

FIG. 84. Fixing of a forehead latex piece.

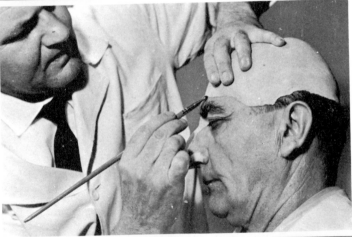

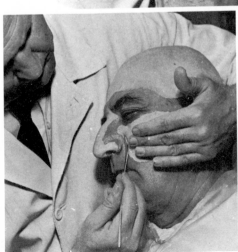

FIG. 85. Fixing of the cheek latex pieces.

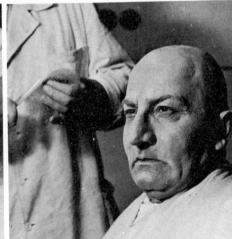

FIG. 86. The mask before fixing the hairpieces.

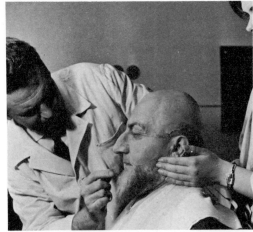

FIG. 87. Fixing the beard.

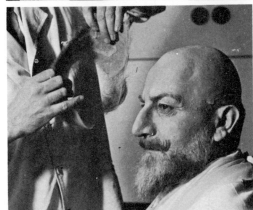

FIG. 88. Fixing the wig.

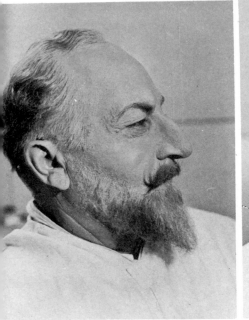
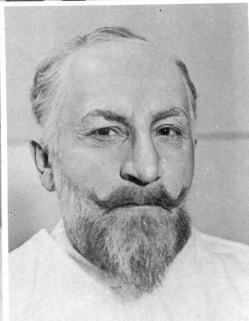

FIGS. 89 and 90, The final mask.

applied to the face with a metal or wooden spatula. It must never be applied with the fingers, because their temperature vulcanizes the paste immediately. The paste is applied bit by bit, starting at the edge of the cast and blending to the skin, taking care that the edge of the cast is completely concealed. The minimum amount is always used as a thicker layer shrinks after drying and makes the edge of the cast even more obvious.

9.2.7. *Make-up for the Foam Latex Casts*

The foam latex pieces are made up with a special rubber mask make-up, which is applied with a small sponge. Sometimes the entire surface of the latex cast is made up with a reddish or reddish-brown make-up which imitates the natural colour of the skin. As a rule, suitable pigments are added to the mixture before curing.

Latex casts are made up with a special make-up, the colour of which is the same as that of the foundation make-up. The special rubber mask make-up does not change its colour on the rubber base, whereas the currently used types of foundation make-up are partly absorbed by the porous cast and their colours turn greyish. If special make-up is not available, the make-up man can apply an insulating layer on the rubber piece and make it up with any kind of foundation make-up. The aqueous solution of polyvinyl alcohol or polyvinyl acetate may be used as an insulating layer. Make-up is applied on the dry insulating layer. However, this layer decreases the porosity and elasticity of the cast and is therefore seldom used.

Special rubber mask make-up may be blended with fatty foundation used for the skin. This, of course, simplifies the make-up man's work. because he can use the same blend for the face as well as for the latex piece. At present, however, only few products may be used for this purpose; pancake is one of them.

The rest of the face is made up after the latex piece has been finished. It is best to use the same type of make-up for the skin as for the artificial pieces; pancake or the mixture of the fatty foundation with the special rubber mask make-up. The special make-up alone is not suitable for the skin as it is absorbed differently by the rubber mask. This makes the skin look unnatural.

There must be perfect colour harmony of the entire face with the latex piece even after the shadows and highlights have been applied. The completed make-up is then lightly powdered (Figs. 91–94).

In film and television studios close co-operation of the make-up man with the cameraman is necessary, as the latter can support the latex piece with the most suitable lighting. Especially in colour film, the false latex parts can be betrayed because of the different absorption of light. This danger increases, when filters inserted in front of light sources are used.

134

FIG. 91. The actor.

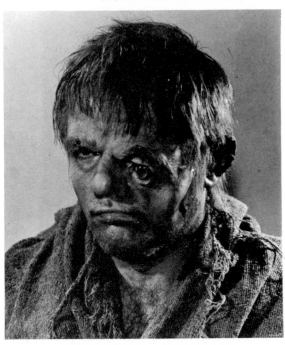

FIG. 92. The actor as Quasimodo.

FIG. 93. The actor.

FIG. 94. Resulting mask.

9.3. REMOVAL AND MAINTENANCE OF THE LATEX PIECES

Before the latex piece is removed, it is moistened with pure ethyl alcohol. The thin edges are carefully lifted with forceps and the cast is easily peeled off the face. The gum is removed from the skin with an alcoholic cleansing lotion, and with an aqueous solution of boric acid. The face is then thoroughly cleaned as usual.

The latex piece must be dipped into acetone immediately after it has been removed from the face. The remains of the adhesive and make-up should be removed with a fine brush. The thin edges must be thoroughly, yet carefully, cleaned because the remaining adhesive would damage the thin texture and they would tear easily. The cleaned cast is then washed in luke-warm, soapy water, rinsed, and dried at room temperature. Organic solvents, such as petrol or benzene, must never be used, because they dissolve rubber and would destroy the latex cast.

9.4. CASTING

It is also possible to make certain types of accessories by casting. As a rule, the cold-setting unfoamed latex mixture is used. It is poured into plaster moulds treated with a soap lubricant.

9.4.1. *Technique*

The plaster mould is filled to the brim with the latex mixture. If the level decreases a little after a while, more mixture must be added. After 20 minutes the mould is turned upside-down, so that the surplus may flow out. There remains a layer on the walls of the mould, the thickness of which depends upon the temperature, the composition of the mixture and on the dryness of the mould. A layer 3–5 mm thick sets at room temperature within 3 hours, or much earlier when it is warmed by an infrared lamp or put into a drying kiln. When the layer is too thin, it is possible to repeat the process until a sufficiently thick cast is obtained. The cast made by this technique faithfully reproduces every detail of the surface of the mould.

The dry casts are elastic, tough, resistant to mechanical damage and they maintain their shape well. They can be coloured in the mixture with the usual pigments or their surface may be painted with oil or distemper colours, with rubber varnish, etc.

Instead of cold-setting latex mixtures, a foam latex mixture can be used. However, sodium fluorosilicate must be added to it as a retardant coagulator. The whipped latex mixture is poured into the mould and after standing for a few minutes the mould is slowly revolved and turned to

137

enable the mixture to enter all its cavities. The excess mixture is then poured out. This process may be repeated as many times as is necessary for obtaining a sufficiently thick layer on the walls of the mould. The cast made from the foam latex mixture must be cured in the drying kiln. This, of course, is unnecessary when the cold-setting mixture is used. The cure of open moulds requires less time than closed moulds. It is advisable to vulcanize one layer after another. Very complicated casts can be prepared by this technique, e.g. casts of the entire head. The inner surface of the moulds must be finished perfectly to achieve seemless casts.

9.5. DIPPING

Dipping is a modification of casting. A mould or a model is dipped into the foam latex mixture or into the cold-setting rubber mixture. After setting or curing, latex forms a coating on the surface of the model or on the inner surface of the mould. The coating can easily be taken off, providing the surface of the mould or model has been treated with a separator. The surface of the mould or of the model must be well finished so that the mixture cannot penetrate into the pores and the coating could be peeled off without difficulty.

Several rules have to be observed if the results are to be satisfactory. A model, either cold or slightly warmed, should be dipped into, and taken out of, the mixture with a slow uninterrupted movement in order to avoid trapping of air bubbles in the rubber coating and in order to obtain a cast with walls of even thickness. After the model has been taken out of the mixture, it should be turned upside-down. The cast is either dried at room temperature or is allowed to cure in the hot-air drying kiln. The process may also be repeated until a sufficient thickness of the layer is achieved. The dried or vulcanized cast is carefully peeled off the model and, if necessary, lightly sprayed with talcum powder to prevent its walls adhering to each other.

The dipping technique is used for making highly elastic, thin, not too complicated casts, grotesque masks with not too marked alterations.

9.5.1. *Composition of the Rubber Mixtures*

The mixtures can be of differing composition, mainly dependent on the kind of latex used. The mixtures are prepared from natural latex and from *Revultex*.

Revultex mixture:

Distilled water	50 parts by weight
Zinc oxide	12

Kaolin	11
Chalk	88
20% aqueous solution of emulsifier	6
10% aqueous solution of potassium hydroxide	2·5
Revultex	1–3

First of all, a paste is prepared by thoroughly mixing all the powdered ingredients, i.e. zinc oxide, kaolin and chalk; water is added and all is stirred until a smooth mixture results. The rest of the distilled water is added to this mixture and stirring is continued. One part by weight of this smooth paste is slowly added to 1–3 parts of *Revultex*. The mixture must be stored in a closed container. It is best to store the prepared paste separately and mix it with *Revultex* shortly before the casting.

Cold-setting latex mixture:

Water	300 parts by weight
20% aqueous solution of Neocal	27
10% aqueous solution of potassium hydroxide	11
Kaolin	50
Chalk	450
Latex	1500

The technique is similar to that mentioned above. Latex, however, contains much more water and more fillers have to be used.

When the foam latex mixture is used for making casts or dipped pieces, the composition may be the same as that of the mixture used for the foam latex accessories.

9.6. LATEX WIGS AND BALD HEADS

Latex wigs and bald heads represent a special kind of rubber accessory for make-up. In film, television, or in the theatre the make-up man must sometimes imitate a completely bald head or make a wig with a high forehead or with a receding hairline. Both must appear convincing, especially in close-ups.

As a rule, suède, which is almost airtight, has been used for this purpose. The impermeability has often been increased by laminated lining, with which the required shape of the head has often been arduously and laboriously constructed. The respiration of the skin has thus been almost completely blocked. Blending with the skin was very difficult, as perspiration, running from beneath such an accessory damaged any make-up. It was always very difficult to imitate bald heads completely. In film, this problem could be solved only by shaving off the hair entirely, because the high sensitivity of the camera would betray the laminated addition at once. In addition, actors usually had other engagements and the shaved hair proved to be the cause of many technical as well as aesthetic problems.

The base of normal wigs is usually made of fine tulle and it blends well with the skin. If, however, a receding hairline, or a high forehead is to be imitated, a suède "cap" must be used under the wig to conceal the actor's own hair and hairline. This is quite satisfactory in the theatre, where there is a constant (often quite long) distance between the actor and the audience, which overcomes minor inaccuracies in the blending of the hairpieces and wigs with the skin, but this technique can never be used in film or television.

However, all the difficulties mentioned above have been overcome within the past few years and at present perfect wigs or completely bald heads are available.

9.6.1. *Latex Wigs*

Latex wig-bases are made of a foam latex mixture of a similar composition as the other latex pieces. The mixture is applied to the plaster model of a head with a spraying pistol, at a pressure of 304–608 N m^{-2}. The structure of the base is affected by the spraying power of the pistol which can be controlled by pressure, and by the distance between the nozzle and the model. The thickness and elasticity of the base can be affected by applying more or less of the mixture to various places of the model. The base is allowed to stand at room temperature for about 30 minutes before it is cured in the kiln, at the most for 1 or 2 hours. After curing is completed the mould is allowed to cool on the model, is removed from it, washed in luke-warm water, and dried at room temperature.

The latex bases are gummed to the actor's head with spirit gum. The actor's hair must be brushed flat to the head, in order not to deform the base (Figs. 95 and 96).

The model heads should be made of plaster and the surface should be carefully treated with a colourless varnish. They should taper towards the "face" and "neck", so that the bases fit the actor's head properly like a bathing cap.

The composition of the mixture is almost identical with that for latex pieces, except for whiting, of which 10–20 per cent is added to the mixtures for the wig-bases. No stabilizers are used in these mixtures, otherwise the procedure is the same as with the other latex pieces. The latex bases do not block the normal respiration of the skin. They are easily put on the head, fit very well and do not require any preliminary preparations of the actor's hair, except sleek brushing. According to the

140

FIGS. 95 and 96. LATEX BALD HEAD

FIG. 95. The actor

FIG. 96. Complete baldness achieved by the use of the latex piece.

141

composition, or rather to its components, the bases can be made of different elasticity, softness and porosity. They do not reflect light and they can be coloured to any required shade by adding the most suitable pigments to the mixture. They can be used in any type of film. Because they are very elastic, they need not be made to measure. They are usually made in three sizes, which fit any shape of head. Their blending with the skin is done in the same way as with the other latex pieces. It is possible to knot the hair on them, so that wigs with a markedly receding hairline appear quite natural, even in close-ups. The hair can be drawn through the base and thus imitate a natural growth from the "skin"; this is important when short and thinning hair is required, through which the "skin" should be seen.

The base can be lengthened in either direction and can very easily imitate a completely bald head. This is important for the faithful portrayals of well-known authentic men.

9.6.2. *Revultex Wigs and Bald Heads*

Revultex need not be vulcanized and the wig-bases can be made by drying. This is very convenient in comparison with latex.

No ultra-accelerators, or activators are added to the *Revultex* mixture. The mixture, with expanding agents and pigments, is foamed in the mixer and is applied to the plaster model with a pad of cotton wool on a wooden holder. The *Revultex* mixture is applied by even strokes on the entire surface of the model. It is dried at room temperature within a few hours. The thinness of the edges depends largely on the dexterity of the assistant who applies the mixture.

9.6.3. *Dispersions of Plastics*

Wig-bases can also be prepared from plastic dispersions. The technique is simpler than the two mentioned above. Suitably coloured dispersions of plastics are applied with a small brush or a pad of cotton wool to an elastic net stretched on the model of a head. The net should be made of a thin, firm fabric, such as nylon or silk stocking material. It can be stretched on the model of a head or on a glass ball (a lamp-shade, for instance) of suitable size. The dispersion can be applied in as many layers as are required to achieve the most suitable thickness. They set within 15 minutes, and a hair dryer or an infrared lamp may be used for drying.

The properties of bases prepared in this way do not differ considerably from those made of latex or *Revultex*. They are a little less elastic, but this drawback is well compensated by the easy and quick preparation, requiring no special equipment. The dispersion may be coloured in the mixture and any kind of make-up may be used on it. Hair may be drawn through the plastic dispersion base even more easily than through the rubber bases. The dispersions are prepared by mixing polyvinyl acetate dispersion with latex and a suitable emulsifier.

Plastic dispersion mixture:

30% dispersion of polyvinyl acetate	500 ml
Titanium dioxide	50 g
10% emulsifier	5 ml
Latex	600 ml

Titanium dioxide is thoroughly rubbed with the emulsifier and Vulcan pigment. Then a 30 per cent dispersion of polyvinyl acetate is added, the mixture is again mixed well and finally the latex is poured in. The mixture must be stirred well.

10. WIGS, HAIRPIECES, AND HAIR STYLES

HAIRDRESSING is an indispensable part of make-up. It completes the appearance of the actor and sometimes has a decisive influence upon it.

In contemporary plays it is usually sufficient to make-up the actor's own hair in a suitable style without the use of any hairpieces, providing, of course, that the colour, length and thickness of the actor's hair fits the suggested hair style.

Dark hair gains more plasticity and highlights when it is lightly powdered with golden or silver bronze or when the ends of some strands are bleached. A receding hairline may be made up by staining the thinning spots with brown or black mascara. A thinning or a receding hairline may be achieved by applying light-toned fatty foundation to the roots of the hair above the forehead.

Greying temples can be made by applying white mascara mixed with bronze or by hair lacquer of a suitable colour. Uneven streaks of grey hair may be achieved in the same way. If the hair is to be completely grey it must be either tinted or a grey wig must be used.

In certain historic periods the hair style was the dominant feature of the entire appearance. It was also a determining factor of make-up which played only a secondary part in the entire arrangement of the head.

Wigs, half-wigs and other hairpieces such as curls, chignons, toupeés, plaits, beards, switches, beards and eyebrows help to portray the characters of certain historic eras and/or of certain social classes. They also help to make a new hairline and make an alteration in the age of the actors possible. Convincing character make-up can be accomplished successfully without the help of wigs and hairpieces.

A good make-up artist has to be also a good wig-maker, so that he can make or supervise the making of many kinds of hairpieces which are required for the complete make-up. The chief make-up artist should always make the wigs for the leading actors personally.

10.1. HUMAN HAIR

Wigs and other hairpieces are made mainly of human hair.

Hair grows from the *hair follicles* in the corium. The *root of the hair* ends in the *hair bulb* which is lodged in the *hair follicle*. When the hair is of considerable length the follicle extends into the subcutaneous tissue. The hair follicle commences on the surface of the skin with a funnel-shaped opening, and passes inwards in an oblique or curved direction — the latter in curly hairs — to become dilated at its deep extremity, where it corresponds with the hair bulb. The ducts of one or more sebaceous glands open into the follicle near its free extremity. At the bottom of each hair follicle there is a small, conical, vascular eminence or *papilla;* it is continuous with the dermic layer of the follicle. The hair follicle consists of two coats — an outer or dermic, and an inner or epidermic.

The inner coat adheres closely to the root of the hair and consists of two layers, named respectively the outer and inner root-sheaths. The inner root-sheath consists of three or four layers of cells of different character.

The *hair bulb* is moulded over the papilla and is composed of polyhedral epithelial cells. As they pass upwards into the root of the hair these cells become elongated and spindle-shaped. The portion of the hair projecting from the surface of the skin is called the shaft, which consists of the medulla, the cortex and the cuticle. The *medulla* is usually absent from the fine hairs covering the surface of the body and commonly from those of the head. The *cortex* constitutes the chief part of the shaft; its cells are elongated and are united to form flattened fibres which contain pigment granules in dark hair and air in white hair. The *cuticle* consists of several layers of flat scales which overlap one another from below. The scales are barely visible even under a microscope and the surface of the shaft looks quite smooth. The minute slits and channels between the scales are filled with hair grease which is produced by the sebaceous gland and which lubricates the hair. The right amount of grease keeps the scales pressed together. The hair is then lustrous, elastic and resistant against elongation and breaking.

Dead hair is permanently separated from the sebaceous gland and therefore cannot be supplied with the usual amount of grease. When such hair is washed and degreased repeatedly it loses its lustre and elasticity, the scales peel off, the cortex fibres separate and the hair breaks easily under a very slight mechanical strain, such as combing, for instance.

This is the main difference between alive and dead hair, from which wigs are made. This difference should be kept in mind as it is very important for the maintenance of wigs and hair pieces. The hair is usually degreased during the process of preparation and so the successive treatment must be very careful not to loosen the scales even more and thus completely deprive the hair of its lustre and elasticity.

The extreme outer membrane of the hair is the *epicuticle*. It is very sensitive to chemical influence such as soap, shampoo, etc. The epicuticle is very important for tinting and bleaching of hair. It is, however, missing in the dead hair and so the wig-maker never encounters it.

The hair used for wig-making can be either cut, fallen out or torn out. A microscopic examination shows clearly which hair is cut and which is torn, or has fallen out, by the different shape of the endings of the respective hairs. Cut hair has a smooth sharp ending, the hair that has fallen out has a club-shaped root. The hair that has been torn out keeps the original shape of the root with a small cavity at the bottom in the place of papilla. Human hair is very strong, stronger than metals, such as lead, zinc, aluminium and copper. It is very elastic, and soft. One single hair lifts over 100 g, a plait of hair can lift 50 kg; this was already recognized in ancient times and bow strings were made of women's plaits.

10.2. TYPES OF HAIR

Hairpieces are chiefly made of healthy, straight or slightly wavy, human hair. Curly hair is not suitable for wig-making. For the preparation of eyebrows and beards animal hairs are used. The worldwide fashion of short hair caused a great lack of human hair of suitable length.

Hair differs in colour, thickness, toughness, shape and length. The following kinds are mainly used for making wigs and other hairpieces.

Central European hair, sometimes called *Czech hair*, has the best quality. It is soft, straight or wavy, available in all natural colour shades ranging from white and pale blonde to black. Any kind of wig or hairpiece can be made of it.

Scandinavian hair is very soft and straight, and is used chiefly for children's wigs. It is available in light colours.

Italian hair is used for making character wigs of medium length and for women's wigs, curled hairpieces and plaits. It is coarser, straight or wavy, and available in various lengths. It is bleached to make it finer. It is sometimes blended with Central European hair.

Chinese (export) hair is straight, dark, thick and coarse. It is used for making special historic and exotic wigs. It is sometimes blended with finer kinds of hair. When crêped, it is used for making beards.

Vietnam hair is thicker than Central European or Italian hair but finer than Chinese hair. It is very dark.

10.2.1. *Animal Hair*

Wigs and hairpieces can also be made of animal hair, or of a blend of animal and human hair.

Yak hair is the mane of the Tibetan yak. It is very tough, white, grey or black. The structure of the filaments is different from the shafts of human hair. Yak hair contains more keratin and is much coarser. The surface of the hair has an uneven structure and the hair is crêped. It is used for making thick, long beards and moustaches. It is also added to Chinese hair. The beards made of this blend of hair have quite a natural appearance.

Goat mane has lighter yellow or grey shades. The hairs are straight and coarse and are added to Chinese hair for making beards, and to the other types of the human hair for making character wigs.

Persian wool is a very fine and lustrous material. It is either white or greyish. It is used for making Renaissance wigs.

Horse hair is straight, thick and of different colours. It is very rarely used alone. It is usually added to Chinese hair for making grotesque or fairy-tale wigs and beards, when it is necessary to maintain unusual shapes of wigs or hair peices.

10.2.2. *Synthetic Hair*

Not all wigs are made of genuine hair, either of pure human or of a blend of human and animal hair. Recently synthetic fibres such as nylon were used. These fibres are very easily tinted to various colour shades. They have lustre and sheen and can be manufactured in any length and strength. It is possible to make any number of wigs of absolutely identical colour such as are necessary for ballet shows, fairy-tale films and fantastic plays.

Synthetic wigs must not be set with hot curling irons. It is advisable to lightly dampen the ends of the hair, set or reset it with curling pins, and dry it in a stream of not too warm air.

10.2.3. *Wool*

In antique or fantastic plays, when uniform artistic style has to be maintained, specially treated, curled wool is used for wigs and beards. The strands are knotted or glued onto the base.

10.3. WIGS AND HAIRPIECES

Wigs and hairpieces for film, television and theatre are all made by the same technique. There are, however, minor differences in the materials used as foundations or bases. The bases for television or film wigs are made of fine, silk tulle, whereas theatre wigs are knotted on a coarser net foundation made chiefly of cotton tulle and fine linen, because the actor perspires a lot on the stage and the fine wig bases would very soon be damaged.

Tinting of film and television wigs must be very subtle and natural looking, together with the construction of the hairline. Lighter hair is usually used for the hairline. It must not be knotted in a sharp, straight line, which would appear very unnatural. In the theatre, where distance must be taken into account, the wigs and other hairpieces can be made of darker hair.

Wigs have to be fixed on the actor's head with the same care and skill in the theatre as they are in film and television, in order to achieve a quite imperceptible blending of the edges of the wig base with the skin. Careless fixing of the wig and other hairpieces would mar the effect of make-up, and might even disturb the actor himself, as well as his colleagues, during the performance. Wigs and other hairpieces must be well kept and carefully cleaned, otherwise perspiration and daily use would very soon damage them.

Wigs, partial wigs, toupeés, beards, moustaches and eyebrows are made by knotting the hair on a fine silk base, whereas switches, postiches, chignons and plaits are loose strands of hair, tightly fastened at one end.

The wig base is made of silk ribbons, firm gauze, muslin or nylon. A perfect wig must blend quite imperceptibly with the skin on the forehead and temples. The best material for wig bases for film use is therefore fine, yet very firm nylon tulle, which fully meets the above-mentioned demands. Silk tulle can be treated by a solution of synthetic resins in an organic solvent to make it firmer. The hardened resins give the tulle more firmness without changing its texture and transparency. Only the best and properly finished material should be used for wig bases, because wigmaking is a slow process, using mostly natural hair which is quite expensive, and it is the quality of the base that determines the durability of the wig.

Beards, moustaches and eyebrows are knotted mainly on tulle, sideburns on tulle or battiste, and toupeés are knotted on silk ribbons and tulle.

Wigs usually cover the hair and the hairline completely or reach as far as the petrosal bone behind the ears, where they blend with the actor's own hair. The colour of the hair must, of course, match.

Half-wigs for men and women are combined with their own hair so as to emphasize all the natural parts of their hairdressing. In some cases when it is not necessary to change or conceal the hairline in the front with a full wig, a half-wig forming a new hairline in the central part of the forehead and covering the hair on the crown of the head, may be used. The actor's own hair is blended with the half-wig at the temples. A toupeé is used to cover the crown of the head, where many men have bald spots or thin hair.

Back half-wigs are used when the actor has thin or short hair at the back of the head, while the front hair can be set into the required hair-do These half-wigs are fitted to the crown of the head and they cover the back of the head completely. The actor's own hair is again blended with the wig or can be combined with other hairpieces at the crown of the head.

Smaller hairpieces are also used to enhance the hairline; these are fitted close to the hairline.

10.3.1. *Measuring the Head*

Well-fitting wigs must be made to measure. Six dimensions of the head must be measured (Fig. 97).

1. *The circumference* — the head is measured for size as for a hat.

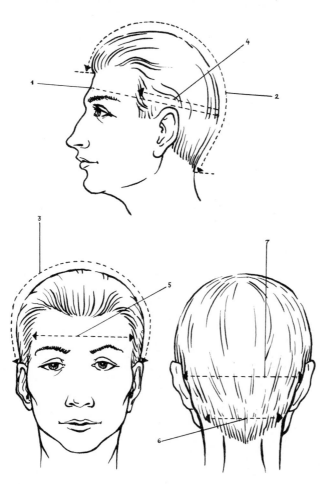

FIG. 97. Measuring the head for a wig. Above: 1. Circumference; 2. Front to back; 4. From temple to temple. Left bottom: 3. Side to side; 5. Forehead. Right bottom; 6. Nape of the neck; 7. The breadth of the head between the ears is measured for a half-wig.

2. *Front to back* — for a full wig it is measured from the lowest point of the hairline on the forehead to the hairline at the nape; for a three-quarter wig it is sufficient to measure to the apex at the back of the head.

3. *Side to side* — from the hairline above the ear to the crown of the head and down to the hairline on the other side.

4. *From temple to temple* — this measurement is taken from the outermost hairline from one temple to the other.

5. *Forehead* — measured from the hairline at the temples.

6. *Nape of the neck* — the hairline at the nape of the neck is measured for a full wig, and the breadth of the head between the ears at the back for a half-wig.

The hairline is then marked with a liner starting at the temples and showing all its irregularities. If a new hairline is to be made, it is traced with a liner on the forehead, a strip of tissue paper or a transparent plastic sheet is then placed on the forehead, and the new hairline is carefully copied onto it. The strip is cut carefully along the hairline. The measurements are then transferred to a wig-maker's block, on which the shape of the wig together with its base and with the possible new hairline, is drawn.

10.3.2. *Wig-making*

The strands of hair containing two to five hairs are knotted on a fabric or a tulle base with a special hooked wig-maker's needle.

The wig must correspond with the character portrayed, the thickness of the wig and the type of knotting being as important as the kind and colour of the hair used. A wig should always be light, airy and not too thick. The shape of the wig, its thickness and the lie of the hair strands must match the proportions of the actor's face. An appropriate wig completes the make-up and sets the age, expression and size of the actor's face.

The colour of the hair is also a very important factor. Softer colours can be used for film and television wigs. Some strands of hair can be slightly bleached to add greater plasticity to the hair-do. Lighter hair is usually knotted on the hairline as it is softer and more natural, and blends better with the skin. White and light coloured wigs used for night scenes in filming should have a lot of sheen, because lighting often gives white coloured hair a dull flaxen tone. Some kinds of synthetic hair have a very faint green hue. White or violet lighting makes the unnatural shade more marked and the final colour effect is distorted.

10.3.3. *How to Set a Wig*

The hair is cut to the required length. Curling irons or curling pins can be used for the final setting. Stiffeners, either liquid or paste, may sometimes be added to the water used for dampening the ends of the hair before curling to maintain the hair-do in position, so as to avoid unnecessary resetting. When the hair is completely dry, it is combed and brushed into the desired shape. The final hair-do is usually sprayed with hair lacquer to fix the hair and give it more lustre. The tulle base of the wig must never be moistened or stained with fixatives, lacquers or oil, because the tulle edge could not be gummed properly to the forehead.

10.3.4. *Fixing a Wig*

The wig must be fitted exactly to the new hairline which was outlined on the actor's forehead before the wig was made. The wig must fit closely to the head so as not to distort its proportions. The actor's own hair must be combed tightly to the head. Women must have the hair either brushed up to the crown of the head, or evenly spread over its back. The hair is fastened tightly with a tulle ribbon which also serves as a foundation for fixing the wig with hairpins or clips at the back of the head. The tulle edges of the wig base are gummed mainly on made-up skin; in some cases, however, when no make-up is used, the wig is fixed on skin entirely free from grease. As a rule, make-up is applied up to the hairline where it is carefully powdered. Gum is applied to the skin with a fine brush; it must never be applied to the tulle edge of the wig. The wig is then carefully fitted. Before the gum is applied, the edges of the wig are lifted a little, great care being taken not to stretch or damage them. The edges must be kept clean, free from the remains of gum, make-up or grease. The tulle edge is gently pressed to the gummed skin with a dry powder puff or a slightly moist buff. If necessary, a little powder may be applied to conceal highlights caused by gum. It is advisable, however, not to touch the tulle edge at all with make-up.

10.3.5. *Cleaning and Maintenance of Wigs and Hairpieces*

Perspiration, gum and the remains of make-up must always be carefully removed from all hairpieces, with a mixture of organic solvents that remove dirt, but do not harm the finish of the tulle base. The tulle base of beards and eyebrows can be immersed in the solvents and the remains of gum can be removed with a brush. Wigs, however, must be cleaned much more carefully, because the hair must not come into contact with the solvents, for they would degrease the hair and it would lose its elasticity and lustre. The hair would split at the ends and break easily. The remaining gum and make-up must be removed only with a brush moistened with the solvent mixture. Quite clean, dry wigs and other hairpieces are then combed and brushed to their original shape and kept well protected from light and dust for further use.

10.3.6. *Beards, Moustaches, Whiskers and Sideburns*

Beard is stronger and tougher than hair, and for making false beards and moustaches tougher kinds of hair are therefore used, such as Chinese hair in combination with yak or goat mane, either in its natural state, crêped or after special treatment.

Beards and similar hairpieces are knotted on tulle or on other kinds of fine-textured fabric. The required shape is obtained by trimming the hairpiece before gumming it to the face.

Sometimes, however, the edges of beards and moustaches are too thickly knotted or the beardline must be altered during filming. In such cases short loose crêpe hair is stuck along the beardline to make it appear absolutely natural. This is usually done in the area of the mouth, where the hairpiece tends to come off at the edges because of the lively play of the facial muscles.

Loose beards and other facial hair growth can also be made by using strands of crêpe hair gummed straight to the face. A suitable strand of crêpe hair is held in the left hand between the thumb and the index finger. First of all it is well brushed and trimmed to the desired length, then it is ruffled a little at the upper end and gummed to the face. It must not form a sharp line. The strands are fixed with spirit gum starting at the chin and advancing to the temples, where the loose beard is blended with the hair. The loose strands must always be placed on the face in the natural direction of beard growth. The same technique is applied for moustaches and eyebrows. For this purpose wavy crêpe hair is preferred to other kinds of hairs. The beard is then trimmed and, if desired, it can be curled with thin beard-curling tongs. To fix its shape properly and to protect it from moisture it is advisable to finish the beard with a thin solution of shellac applied very subtly with a brush (Figs. 98–100).

Spirit gum is nowadays replaced by plastic paste for the above-mentioned purpose. The technique of application is described below.

An unshaven face is made by sticking short, loose pieces of hair on the face. Plastic paste blended with foundation make-up is applied onto the whole beard area. The short crêpe hair is applied with a hair brush by dabbing it on this base. The hair is first applied to the chin and to the upper lip, then to the throat and cheeks. It is much better to use the paste than spirit gum, as the plastic paste does not glisten, can be blended with the foundation, and the process is much quicker (Figs. 101 and 102).

10.3.7. *Eyebrows*

The colour of the eyebrows, their shape and the way they grow, greatly affect the expression of the face. If it is impossible to obtain the required shape by brushing and applying make-up, knotted or loose eye-

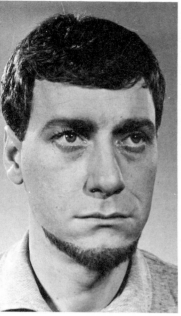
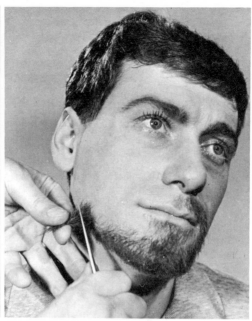
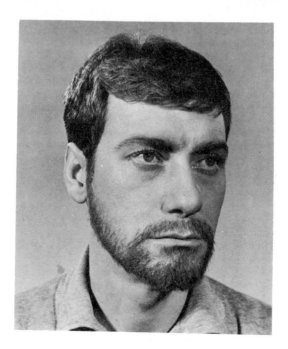

FIGS. 98–100. Fixing of loose beards.

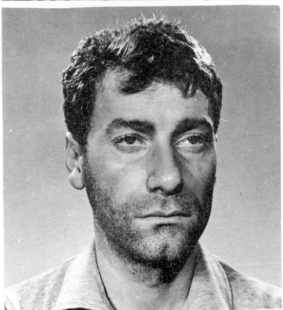

FIGS. 101 and 102. Several days' growth of beard. Short loose pieces of crêpe hair are applied with a hair brush by dabbing it on the beard area covered with a thin layer of plastic paste

154

brows have to be used. The technique for fixing loose eyebrows is the same as for the unshaven face.

10.4. STYLES OF HAIR-DO

The make-up artist must have a basic knowledge of the development of hair styles and their changes through the ages. Some hair styles were short-lived, whereas some styles spread from their country of origin to many others and certain characteristic features of some styles can be traced through the ages to the present style of hair dressing.

The most important historic periods for the make-up artist are those filled with dramatic events which are still the source of artistic inspiration to many playwrights. The make-up man is often given the task of designing and making a complete mask historically faithful in all details. As has already been mentioned, the coiffure is an essential part of the mask and the following paragraphs are intended to acquaint the make-up artist with some facts from the history of hair styles.

10.4.1. *Ancient Greece*

The most cultured nation in Europe in ancient times was Greece. A typical feature of Greek culture was a refined artistic feeling for the beauty of the human body. This was proved in the meticulous care with which the ancient Greeks cultivated their physical charm and appearance. They devoted great attention to hairdressing, men at that time perhaps more than women. Men used fragrant hair pomades for their elaborate hair-dos. They often coiled their hair above the forehead and fastened it with ribbons or gold bands to form braids at the back of their heads and sometimes they let their hair fall freely to their shoulders in a mass of curls. They also wore plaits and braided twists and switches. They sometimes wore moustaches. The slaves in Greece, men and women, wore their hair short. Later on, men's hair-dos became less and less elaborate; only young boys wore long hair which had to be cut short as soon as they joined the army. In the city of Sparta, older men wore long hair, whereas the hair of young men was short. Older men also wore carefully trimmed beards, and young men preferred to be clean-shaven (Fig. 103).

Women enhanced the beauty of their faces, shoulders and throats by wearing elaborate hair styles. They coiled their rich tresses on the crown of their heads, a style which has been more or less popular ever since. The fashionable colour of hair at that time was blonde. Much later on, however, as the result of expeditions into Asia and closer contact with Asiatic tribes, darker hair was preferred.

155

Fig. 103. Greece.

10.4.1.1. *The time of Alexander the Great.* Alexander the Great conquered many countries in the Mediterranean as well as in what is now known as the Middle East and penetrated as far as India. Greece at that time became very rich and sophisticated. The situation was also apparent in the complicated and elaborate care of appearance, noticeable particularly in the hair styles of women. They wore their hair piled high on their heads, twisted and braided very intricately, so that the coiffure governed the entire appearance. A hair-do very commonly used was one in which the hair was divided into a large number of strands with many partings (Fig. 104).

Young girls wore their hair twisted either at the crown or at the nape of the neck in a way that is popular even today. Men wore their hair shorter and shorter and were clean-shaven. Long hair and beards were the signs of thinkers and philosophers.

FIG. 104. The time of Alexander the Great.

10.4.1.2. *Rome*. Two historical periods of entirely different political character can be distinguished in the history of ancient Rome – the Republic and the Empire. In the time of the Republic, Rome was strongly influenced by Greeks just as many other city states and countries in the Mediterranean of that time. The first barbers and hairdressers that came to Rome in the third century B.C. were Greeks. They introduced short hair to Rome; until then cutting of hair was very unusual. Men had long hair and beards or were clean-shaven. Women also adopted the Greek hair style and coiled their hair first at the nape of the neck and then high at the crown.

In the Empire, men had short hair brushed to the forehead in a fashion that even nowadays is known as the Titus haircut. During the reign of Emperor Hadrian a long beard was the latest fashion. It was modern until the reign of Emperor Constantine, who was clean-shaven, and so beards were abandoned again.

The hair styles of women changed very rapidly at that time. They were very complicated, elaborate and the latest fashion in hairdressing was so important that women present at the banquets of the Roman empresses were allowed to change the hair-do even during the banquet (Figs. 105 and 106).

Bleaching was very common and the lightest shades, admired as the Germanic women's hair, were the most popular. Switches, chignons and postiches were largely used for elaborate hair styles. The complicated

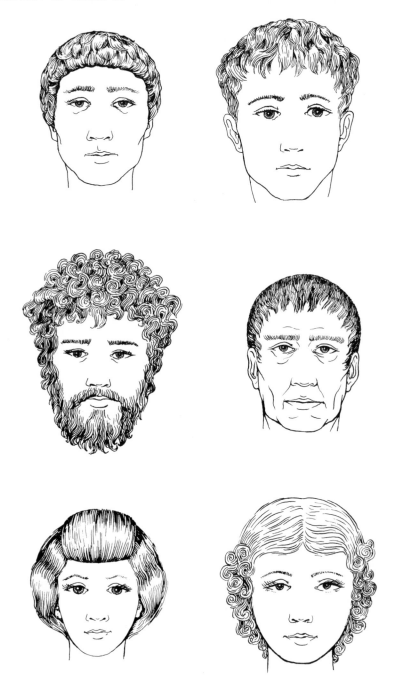

FIGS. 105 and 106. Rome.

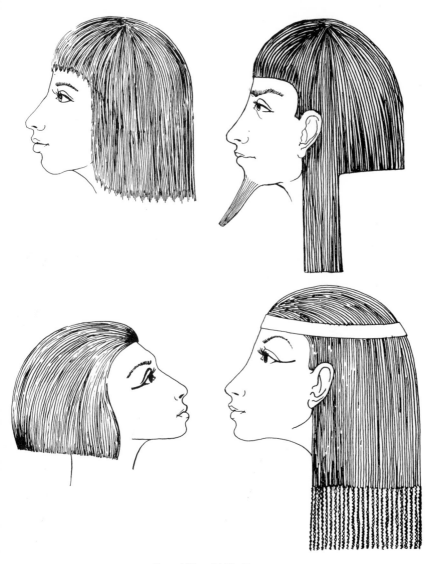

FIGS. 107 and 108. Egypt.

hair-dos were considered as a sign of frivolity at the time of the Republic, but at the time of the Empire were adopted by the majority of women of noble birth. Women started to use make-up, perfumes, fragrant vegetable extracts and oils, and frequently visited luxurious baths. They watched their diet very carefully and had regular massages to keep their body fresh, slim and beautiful.

159

FIGS. 109 and 110.
Oriental hair styles.

160

The Romans took very sophisticated care of their bodies. Luxurious and excellently equipped baths, preserved in many countries, witness to the present day their endeavour to enhance their charm and beauty.

10.4.1.3. *Egypt and the Middle East.* The Egyptians, men as well as women, had short hair. They used wigs for special occasions, such as religious festivals and state banquets. The wigs and false beards, also frequently used, were made of human as well as of animal hair or of vegetable fibres. The Egyptians tinted their hairpieces with red, white or green herbal extracts (Figs. 107 and 108).

The Babylonians, Assyrians and Persians preferred their own long hair and beards, which they curled and hennaed. Wigs were used very seldom and only by women (Figs. 109 and 110).

10.4.1.4. *The Jews.* The Jews preferred very simple hair styles. They usually covered their heads with cloth or veils. The nomadic tribes also had simple hair-dos and they wore beards. The typical feature of a Jewish face were the side-whiskers, which many orthodox Jews wear even nowadays. Women had the hair parted in the middle and they either fastened it

Fig. 111. The Jews.

with a ribbon or let it loosely onto their shoulders. They veiled their heads too (Fig. 111).

10.4.1.5. *The Celts and Teutons.* The Celts of the Bronze Age wore long hair falling to their shoulders. Men were either clean-shaven or wore beards. Women braided the hair in plaits or fastened it with ribbons at the nape of the neck, or combed it to the crown of the head, where they clipped it together and let it fall down in a form of a pony tail, a fashion that was popular not so many years ago.

Later on, in the Iron Age, the Celts bleached their naturally fair hair to still lighter tones. Men combed their hair back on the neck and noblemen adopted big moustaches and clean-shaven cheeks. Women coiled their hair at the nape of the neck, or combed it to the crown, where they braided it in a style similar to that common in Greece (Fig. 112).

FIG. 112. The Celts.

With the exception of the Saxons, all the Teutonic tribes had long hair. The northern tribes let the hair fall freely to their shoulders, whereas the eastern ones coiled it into a firm bun or twist at the nape of the neck; they very often fixed it with resins to maintain its shape. Later on, approximately in the second century, they abandoned this fashion, most probably because of the spreading influence of Greco-Roman culture, but in some regions of their territory, this fashion was maintained until the sixth century A.D.

The hair style of Teutonic women was very simple. Older women fastened their hair with tuck combs, young girls had loose hair. In spite of the simplicity of style, women devoted great care to the hair; tinting was very common among women as well as among men and a rusty colour was most favoured. The Celts, however, strongly influenced the hair styles of the Teutons (Fig. 113).

162

FIG. 113. The Teutons.

10.4.2. *The Middle Ages; the Franks*

The cultural and political development of Central and Western Europe was greatly influenced by the rapid expansion of the Franks, who by the fifth century A.D. had conquered all the Teutonic tribe as well as the Galls.

The Franks blended quickly with the Galls and they adopted the Gallic fashion, which again was under the strong influence of Rome. Men wore short hair, with the exception of kings, who always had long hair. Women usually wore plaits and later on coiled them into the form of a crown at the top of their heads. They also wore scarves. When the Franks adopted Christianity, women had to cover their heads with scarves whenever they went to church. Scarves and veils thus became an indispensable part of women's clothing (Fig. 114).

10.4.2.1. *The Slavs.* The hair style of the Slavs was very different from those of the Greeks and Romans. Women as well as men had long hair,

163

FIG. 114. The Franks.

FIG. 115. The Slavs.

usually parted in the middle. Women also wore plaits, girls had loose hair, often decorated with floral wreaths. The hair style was affected by the Byzantine fashion. Women frequently wore brow-bands or jewelled diadems. Old women swathed their heads in big scarves. Men wore long beards or very big, long moustaches, young men preferred short beards and moustaches parted in the middle (Fig. 115).

When the Bohemian Slavs became Christians, they had to cut their hair a little shorter, because long hair was considered a sign of paganism. Men cut their hair just below the ears; women, however, retained the original style, until the late Middle Ages.

The nobility and rich citizens adopted the French fashion in the late fourteenth and early fifteenth century. Men had short hair combed in the form of a sleek helmet; they shaved off the hair at the temples and at the ears. Women and girls curled their hair and covered it with long, fine veils or elaborately decorated nets, often made of gold or silver threads.

10.4.2.2. The tenth and eleventh century. Men had short hair, long beards and big moustaches. Younger men were clean shaven. Women still wore scarves and veils and covered their hair almost completely (Fig. 116).

FIG. 116. The tenth and eleventh century.

10.4.2.3. The twelfth and thirteenth century. Women were very fond of plaits at that time. Unmarried girls were allowed to be bareheaded with long hair falling gently to their shoulders. Married and older women swathed their heads in big scarves, which were later adorned with a thin silver or gold band. Gradually the scarves were abandoned and only the band was retained as jewellery. Only old women and nuns kept the

165

FIG. 117. The twelfth century.

FIG. 118. The thirteenth century.

original form of the big scarf, which even today is part of the nun's attire (Figs. 117 and 118).

Men adopted the fashion of longer hair again, curled it at the ends and on the forehead. Country people retained their hair style almost unchanged, so that longer hair was a sign of nobility and of noble birth.

10.4.2.4. *The fourteenth century*. The fourteenth century again revived the fashion of short hair for men's coiffure. They shaved off the hair at the temples and combed the hair in a sleek and extremely simple style. Some men preferred slightly wavy hair, and a beard or a moustache. Women enhanced the soft line of the throat, shoulders and neck by wearing low-cut bodices and by braiding their hair into rich plaits coiled to form a crown at the top of their heads. A very high forehead was considered beautiful at that time and women shaved off quite a lot of their hair at the front and thus disclosed most of their frontal bones. Only spinsters were allowed to wear uncoiled hair (Fig. 119).

10.4.2.5. *The fifteenth century*. The beginning of the fifteenth century stressed the sleek helmet-like men's hair-do still more than the previous

FIG. 119. The fourteenth century.

century. The hair was cut smoothly to the ear-tip and brushed evenly from a full crown to all sides. The second half of the fifteenth century again brought the fashion of longer wavy hair for men (Figs. 120–123).

Women again adopted veils and scarves and almost completely covered their hair, often coiled at the sides of the head, in conical, horn-like formations (Fig. 124).

10.4.3. *The Renaissance*

During the fifteenth century and mainly at its end, a new artistic style, reviving the classical ideal of beauty and arts, strongly influenced the European continent. Women's hair styles were designed individually,

FIG. 120. The fifteenth century.

FIGS. 121, 122 and 123. Men's hair-dos in the fifteenth century (the Gothic style).

FIG. 124. The Gothic swathing.

often by famous painters and artists. The hair was richly adorned with jewels, pearls, ribbons and nets. Men wore long hair and long beards; sometimes they had small moustaches as well.

During the fifteenth century women preferred a conical line in their hair style. Scarves and veils were gradually abandoned and the hair was fastened with clasps, buckles and ornamented hairpins and combs. A high forehead remained modern and the typical posture for portraying at that time was profile, showing the curve of the forehead. Well-kept, rich hair was every woman's greatest pride and much care was devoted to tinting and bleaching, which was chiefly done by exposing the hair to strong sunshine. The use of make-up became a matter of fact at the end of the fifteenth century (Figs. 125 and 126).

In Germany, men preferred a very simple sleek style with short hair combed evenly from the top of the head to the sides and to the forehead. In the thirties of the fifteenth century the hair was so short that it disclosed the ears. All shapes of beard became fashionable again. A thin strip of beard passing from one ear under the chin to the other ear was quite common; the cheeks were clean-shaven. Women wore a high, tightly fastened coiffure. Long plaits were modern around the twenties of the fifteenth century. Completely displayed hair-do was very rare in Germany, where women were very fond of covering their hair with hair-nets.

170

FIGS. 125 and 126. The Renaissance.

In Italy women preferred soft style of loose hair falling to their shoulders. No veils or nets were worn.

At the beginning and during the sixteenth century, men again adopted short hair and beards. A beret was the typical cover of the head for men at that time. Women had their hair combed high at the crown of their heads, as a new fashion of high starched lace piccadills required. High forehead ceased to be fashionable and the hairline returned to its natural

171

area. The hair framed the face again. Girls retained their style of loose, slightly wavy hair. They also braided their hair in plaits entwined with ribbons.

10.4.3.1. *The Spanish fashion.* The typical feature of the Spanish fashion of that time were the rich lace piccadills, starched and tough, Men had their hair cut short, and women brushed it to the top of their heads. Spanish men wore short hair until the seventeenth century when they adopted a more elaborate style of longer hair again. Small moustaches were very popular in Spain in the sixteenth century.

The hair style in Spain was as strict and tough as the fashion of that time. At the beginning of the second half of the sixteenth century women combed their hair up from the temples and neck, and twisted it at the top of their heads. Together with the bigger and higher piccadills the hair-do had to be higher as well. Thanks to the fashion of the big lace collars, of which the women of Spain were very fond, their high hair styles remained unchanged until the seventeenth century, while in the other countries of Europe, women returned to less elaborate hairdress. The Spanish women pinned small hats and jewellery to their almost pyramidal coiffure (Fig. 127).

FIG. 127. The Spanish fashion.

The Spanish fashion was copied in many other European countries. France was also affected by its strict and stylized line for a time, but soon adopted a simpler and softer style of its own; the hair was curled at the temples and above the forehead, in the centre of which the hairline was pointed a little.

10.4.4. *The Seventeenth Century*

At the end of the sixteenth and at the beginning of the seventeenth

172

century men started to wear long, curly hair and very short beards; moustaches were parted in the middle and brushed upwards at the sides.

In Central European countries a simpler fashion prevailed. Men preferred short hair to long, the fashion in beards varied, but the beard was always very tidy and well kept. Peasant people maintained the Gothic hair style almost unchanged. Women's hair style was adapted to the shape and size of the piccadills.

In the first decades of the seventeenth century the Spanish fashion kept its influence on Europe. With the decreasing political influence of Spain in Europe, however, even fashion affected the nobility of Europe less and less, and later on it was France, or rather the French Court, that gradually became the leading power in the European fashion styles.

10.4.4.1. *England in the middle of the seventeenth century.* In the middle of the seventeenth century the long struggle between the king and the people, represented by Parliament, reached its most decisive moments, and England was, for a time, split into two political, cultural and religious groups—the Royalist and the Parliamentarians. The members of these respective groups differed greatly in their ideas as well as in their appearance, which bore marked signs of their beliefs.

The Royalists were gay and pleasure-loving gentlemen, very fashionable and very fond of art, luxury and beauty. They wore long, curled hair and richly adorned clothes that were modern all over the European continent.

The Parliamentarians, on the other hand, were mostly Puritans and they wanted a simpler and plainer form of religion and life, devoid of all luxury. Their dress had a plain cut and was dull in colouring. Their hair was cut shorter and brushed close to the head—the Royalists called them "Roundheads" (Fig. 128). Women also wore very simple dresses

Fig. 128. The Puritans.

without any decorations or jewels, and their hair-do was very strict-looking. They had their hair brushed sleekly back to the nape of their necks, where they coiled it in buns.

The simplicity of the Puritan style of dress and hair-do was an extra-ordinary feature, greatly differing from all the other countries on the continent, where the most decorative baroque style was reaching its climax in architecture as well as in fashion.

10.4.4.2. *The reign of Louis XIV — the baroque style.* In the reign of Louis XIV France stabilized its political and cultural influence over a considerable part of Europe together with which the fashion influence went hand in hand.

The most typical feature of the French fashion of that time is the use of wigs. The wig, was, of course, nothing new in history, for it was used in many countries long before the French revived its use again in the seventeenth century. The Spanish men's style, of short hair, however, had no use for a wig at first, but later on even the Spaniards adopted it. In the first half of the seventeenth century the shape and colour of the wig corresponded with the natural appearance, but later it was a bigger and bigger mass of locks, falling in rich cascades onto the wearer's back, breast and shoulders. Men's wigs were meant to express the power and might of men and to give them the appearance of a lion — a symbol of male strength and beauty. Very light colours were preferred to enhance the likeness with the lion's mane. Wigs were generously powdered with white powder. The wigs of that time must have been very uncomfortable and hot. However, they were certainly very expensive, because they were made of pure curled, human hair.

Women coiled their hair into long, serpent-like curls, which hung loosely on their backs and shoulders. The forehead was framed with soft curls. the top of the head was usually flat and sleekly combed (Figs. 129–132).

Later on, however, the elaborate style of men's wigs affected the soft line of women's hair-do as well. The curls at the temples were maintained, but all the remaining hair was piled high up on the top of the head, where it was brushed to the sides, so that the hair-do was very wide. The pyra-mids of hair had to be reinforced with very elaborate constructions to hold them in an upright position, because otherwise the intricate coils, braids and twists, very often much higher than the head itself, would inevitably collapse.

The common people had shorter hair, falling in soft waves onto the shoulders. Women wore scarves, bonnets or hoods to conceal their hair. Peasant girls wore long plaits.

10.4.5. *The Eighteenth Century*

The eighteenth century is the last stage of the Royal Court fashion

Figs. 129 and 130. The time of Louis XIV (the baroque style).

which is different from that of the townsmen and merchants. This is the century of the political and cultural emancipation of the town-dwellers and merchants, the time of emancipation which came from England and spread to most countries on the European continent after the French Revolution.

175

Figs. 131 and 132. Baroque hair styles.

The financial situation of the French Court was far from prosperous at the beginning of the eighteenth century. Men abandoned elaborate and expensive wigs and set their own hair into simpler hairdress. The medium-length hair was brushed back and fastened at the nape with a ribbon or it was concealed in a small pouch hanging on the back. The fashion was adapted first of all in the army, because the long, loose hair or a wig could not be kept in order or stay put while riding a horse. The hair was also braided in a little plait at the nape and bound with a bow, and brushed sleekly from the forehead. It formed small curls at the temples. The noblemen powdered their hair with white, grey, brown, sometimes even with red and blue powder. Simple, black wigs were worn for riding (Fig. 133).

Fig. 133. The rococo hair style.

Women adopted very low hair-do with exposed forehead. The face was framed with curls at the temples. The hair was powdered. The hair at the back was curled and sometimes braided in plaits. For celebrations, state occasions and banquets, high and elaborate hairdress was still used, propped up with complicated wire constructions, and often styled with various hair-pieces. Hairdressing took several hours and only very wealthy women could afford this. The hair, heavily perfumed and covered with pomade, was not thoroughly combed and brushed or washed for many days and very often not for many weeks! This fashion, however, came to its end with the outbreak of the French Revolution at the end of the eighteenth century. At the end of the eighteenth century, men adopted very simple hair style of loose, medium long hair and clean-shaven faces. Peasant women wore hoods and lightly curled hair, framing the face. Before the French Revolution noble women applied rouge to their cheeks very generously. The cheeks had to contrast vividly with the alabaster white of the rest of the face, generously powdered with white powder. Natural-looking make-up was old-fashioned and was considered as offending. To

177

enhance the pallid face still more, little patches of black silk were applied to the cheeks as beauty-spots.

10.4.6. *The French Revolution*

In the turbulent years of the French Revolution fashion was much simpler than ever before. Laces, elaborate dresses, wigs and pigtails were abandoned. The hair was shortened to medium length, and after the Revolution short curls became the latest fashion (Fig. 134).

FIG. 134. The time of the French Revolution.

10.4.7. *The First Half of the Nineteenth Century*

At the beginning of the nineteenth century, during the reign of Napoleon, men wore short hair again, slightly wavy at the temples. They were clean-shaven save for the sideburns.

Women had rich curls on the entire head. The face was framed with a mass of curls on the forehead and at the temples. The hair was parted in the middle and coiled at the top of the head. Feathers and embroidered or jewelled bow-bands were used to decorate the hair-do (Fig. 135).

After Napoleon's defeat, the French fashion lost its leading position on the continent. Hair styles were simpler, the hair brushed sleekly to the head and coiled at the crown in twists or plaits.

After two decades of political changes and hardship of the Napoleonic wars, Europe finally enjoyed a short period of peace, which was reflected in fashion styles.

Women parted their hair in the middle, coiled it at the temples and at the top of the head in twists or plaits. They also used hairpieces to make

FIG. 135. The first half of the nineteenth century.

their hair thicker. Ribbons were largely used to fasten the plaits at the sides of the face. Curls were very popular at that time and were framing the face at the temples (Fig. 136).

Men wore medium-length hair, slightly wavy. They had clean-shaven cheeks and wore side whiskers; moustaches were becoming popular (Fig. 137).

At the end of the first half of the nineteenth century women simplified their hair-do still more by brushing the hair sleekly over the ears and to the nape of the neck where they twisted it into a bun or a plait.

10.4.8. *The Second Half of the Nineteenth Century. Beginning of the Twentieth Century*

In the fifties of the last century, men's hair styles definitely did away with all the remaining features of the rococo effeminacy. The hair was short, maintaining the natural hairline, parted in the middle or at one side. No curls or waves were worn. Beards and big moustaches parted in the middle were popular; they retained their popularity until the Great War.

179

FIG. 136. The middle of the nineteenth century (Biedermeier).

FIG. 137. The sixties of the nineteenth century (Empire).

Girls arranged their hair simply in curls, fastened with a ribbon at the top of the head. Plaits were also very common.

In the sixties, women still used hairpieces in the form of rich curls falling on their shoulders. In the following decade, the style was again simpler with the hair combed up and fastened with a ribbon. Ears were disclosed and the curls fell at the back or were coiled at the top of the head. The curls were very often combed up above the forehead to frame the face (Fig. 138).

FIG. 138. The seventies of the nineteenth century.

The evening hair-do was simple, too. Only flowers were used as a decoration of the hair.

In the nineties simplicity still prevailed. At the end of the century, however, the styles were getting more and more complicated and elaborate. Hairpieces were lavishly used again, to create rich and voluble hair-dresses, false plaits were fastened to the top of the head, masses of tiny

FIG. 139. The eighties of the nineteenth century.

181

curls, called frou-frou, fell to the forehead. The continental fashion of the end of the nineteenth century and of the beginning of the twentieth century was markedly affected by the new very decorative artistic style coming from France, called Art Nouveau (Figs. 139–141).

FIG. 140. The Art Nouveau.

This fashion changed shortly before the Great War. Women again adopted simpler and smaller hair-dos, which copied the classical shapes. The War, however, deeply affected life in Europe and fashion had to be adapted to the changed living conditions. Simplicity in clothing as well as in hairdressing was typical for this period. The hair was combed back in soft waves and coiled in a small bun at the nape of the neck.

10.4.9. *The Twenties of the Twentieth Century*

Shortly after the end of the Great War, women bobbed their hair very short. This was quite a revolutionary act in the history of feminine hair styles, as never previously would women have dared to cut their hair short and thus invade men's centuries' old privilege of being able to wear short hair whenever they wanted to.

The political events shortly before and after the Great War, bringing

FIG. 141. Men's fashion at the time of Art Nouveau.

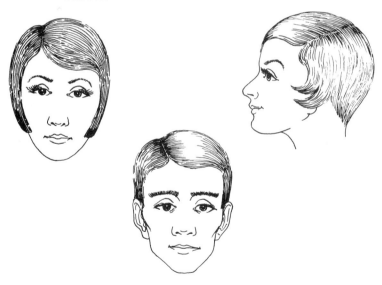

FIG. 142. The twenties of the twentieth century.

emancipation of women and then the war itself, influenced them so much, that as an open demonstration of their equal rights with men, the fashion of bobbed hair swept through Europe and North America and firmly established its position for the next forty years (Fig. 142).

183

INDEX